T · H · E
BEST
LITTLE
BEADING
B · O · O · K

BY WENDY SIMPSON CONNER

INTERSTELLAR

TRADING & PUBLISHING COMPANY
LOS ANGELES, CALIFORNIA

THE BEST LITTLE BEADING BOOK
ISBN 0-9645957-0-2
Library of Congress Catalog Card Number: 95-94215
SAN: 298 - 5829
EMAIL: Interstlr@aol.com / Visit our Website: www.interstellarpublishing.com
For Orders or Questions: (310) 247-8154

All illustrations by Wendy Simpson Conner
Black and white photography by Wendy Simpson Conner
Color photography by Don Brandos
Printed in the United States of America

FIRST PRINTING: APRIL, 1995
SECOND PRINTING: SEPTEMBER, 1995
THIRD PRINTING: JUNE, 1997
FOURTH PRINTING: OCTOBER, 1997
FIFTH PRINTING: APRIL, 1998
SIXTH PRINTING: FEBRUARY, 1999
SEVENTH PRINTING: JANUARY, 2000
EIGHTH PRINTING: OCTOBER, 2000
NINTH PRINTING: JULY, 2001
TENTH PRINTING: JANUARY, 2002
ELEVENTH PRINTING: SEPTEMBER, 2002
TWELFTH PRINTING: MAY, 2003
THIRTEENTH PRINTING: APRIL, 2004
FOURTEENTH PRINTING: MAY, 2005

ACKNOWLEDGMENTS:
To Jennie, who started it all;
To Joni and Paul for putting up with my intensity;
And, most of all, to my mother, Priscilla Simpson,
whose patience and talent has greatly influenced my life.
My heartfelt gratitude goes to my aunt, Perlso Lewis,
for taking such good care of my grandmother's beadwork;
and to Phyllis Shealy, for her love and goodness.

Introduction

As a girl, my grandmother, Jennie, did lovely Victorian beadwork. When she was twelve, she came to America. She was fortunate to obtain a position as a domestic with Anna Held, a popular stage actress and first wife of Flo Ziegfeld, of the Ziegfeld follies. It did not take long for the Ziegfelds to see Jennie's great talent with beading, and to have her designing beadwork for Anna and the other members of the show. Jennie was beading and designing gowns, accessories, pictures, lampshades, and much more.

She could make her own lace (she made her own wedding dress by hand); she beaded flapper dresses, she made shoulder pads. She was truly ahead of her time with the sophistication of her designs (There are photographs of some of her work on the following pages).

Her daughter, my mother, carries on the tradition. She sews, needlepoints, does embroidery, and is extremely gifted with all she creates.

My father was a very talented artist — he could reproduce almost any illustration he saw.

With such a legacy, it seemed natural that I, too, would be artistic. A designer by trade, I've worked in the visual arts for many years.

My love affair with beads is a true genetic affliction. One of my earliest memories is playing with my grandmother's button and bead boxes. In the 1960's. My girlfriends and I would sit at school and string love beads into necklaces and wire bead rings.

In the 70's, we graduated to beading leather, macrame, and other similar crafts.

By the time the 90's arrived, it was apparent that I would never tire of my love of beads. I am a self-admitted "bead addict" or "bead-a-holic". I admit I have absolutely no will-power when it comes to beads — it's very hard for me to walk away from what I know to be a rare and unusual find. If given the choice between lunch or beads, I usually skip the lunch and buy the beads.

I worked in the television industry as a designer when I lived in Los Angeles, then, in the early 80's, I started teaching a vocational jewelry making class for the San Diego Community Colleges (I now teach in several adult education programs). I opened a bead store in San Diego, California (The Bead Centre), and I write for several bead-related magazines (If you like my articles in *Lapidary Journal*, then you'll love this book).

My students share my love of beads and bead work — the classes are workshops where wonderful ideas and beautiful things flourish.

In large part, this book is for my students, who asked all the right questions, and pushed me to write this book. The one comment I hear the most is the fact that many bead books only cover one or two techniques, and that to buy every book would cost a small fortune. Also, there's nothing that teaches my original classroom projects, or my grandmother's designs. I started out by creating my own handouts and brochures for my students to fill in the gaps. As these grew in number, I received requests to bind them, and include photos. This book is a long time in the making. When I was on maternity leave with my daughter, this was going to be my "six-week project". Twelve years later, it's finally done. I've tried to cover every aspect I can think of. I've included (as a friend noted) everything but the kitchen sink.

Some of the projects in this book are adaptations of traditional techniques, some are my interpretations, and some are original ideas. I'm one of those people who looks at something and says, "If it can be done this way, why not also do it that way?" I find it an artistic challenge to create . . . I may tire of a technique after one or two pieces, but for me the fun lies in the conquering. When I make earrings, the first one is a fun adventure. The second one seems like work, because I've tread that road already!

This book is designed to be a work book — there are instructions on how to do different techniques, a picture glossary, idea sections, and lots more. It's bound in this manner so that it will lay flat as you work. It is this size so that you can put it in your bead box and carry it along on trips.

My goal is to provide you with ideas and examples, and to make them obtainable and within everyone's ability. Anyone can create what is in this book. Because most people learn best from visuals (in addition to descriptions), this book has many diagrams and illustrations. For both beginners and more advanced bead artists, I hope this is helpful.

I start with the simplest and work up to the complex. I emphasize that yes, there are standard tools and rules, but also there's the insights that come when you realize that you must be flexible in your ideas and ways of seeing, and be open to new solutions for creative problems.

Everyone has talent. Sometimes we all stop ourselves from being creative because it seems like such a strange new place to go. But there is no greater thrill than when you have made something wonderful, and people stop you on the street to tell you so! Enjoy what you create, and feel that sense of achievement that you've created a true work of art.

Jennie's Beadwork

My grandmother, Jennie's, bead-work was so special and so ahead of its time, that I had to include it in this book. Her patterns were very unique. I've included the instructions for many of these projects.

My grandmother, Jennie

Anna Held, first wife of Flo Ziegfeld. My grandmother designed many costumes and jewelry for her.

Irridescent glass necklace and memory wire bracelet set designed for Anna Held

Cluster necklace made of glass beads. Looks like flowers.

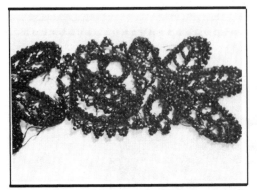

Beaded sleeve edging done in the Passementerie style (beaded on a cord).

Detail of beaded dress

Beaded belt

Circular lace earrings

This dress was hand-sew and hand-beaded, with a detachable snap-in lining.

Crystal necklace

Fragments of a lampshade fringe

Purse beaded with steel
seedbeads

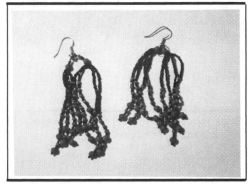

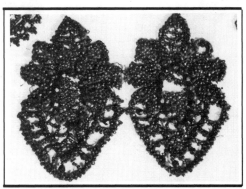

Red and black crystal earrings worn by Ziegfeld
Follies for production number

Appliques done in Passamenterie technique
(beaded on a cord)

Beaded picture (my grandmother did this to tease my grandfather, because he was always busy).

Shoulder pad

Choker with clasp made of beads

Same necklace as left, but showing braided effect of front of necklace.

Jet and crystal necklaces

Sleeve edging done in Passamenterie technique

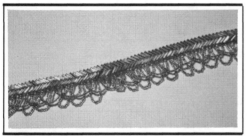

Beaded choker

Beaded accents on belt

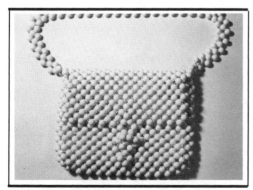

My grandmother didn't make this, but this is a beaded purse from the sixties

I made a matching changepurse when I was 11.

Measurements - Millimeters / Inches

We are so used to measuring in inches, that we are completely thrown when someone says "metric system". Most beads are measured by millimeters (metric), which sends us scurrying for that "other ruler" when confronted with the task of figuring out how many beads we need. This reference should help. Keep in mind that millimeters and inches don't translate evenly. Usually you have to round up or down to even it out to whole beads.

		Bead Size				
Inches	Millimeters	2mm	4mm	6mm	8mm	10mm
1"	± 25 mm	appx. 13	appx. 6	appx. 4	appx. 3	appx. 2½
8"	± 203 mm	appx. 102	appx. 51	appx. 34	appx. 25	appx. 20
10"	± 254 mm	appx. 127	appx. 64	appx. 42	appx. 32	appx. 26
12"	± 305 mm	appx. 153	appx. 76	appx. 51	appx. 38	appx. 31
16"	± 415 mm	appx. 208	appx. 104	appx. 69	appx. 52	appx. 42
20"	± 508 mm	appx. 254	appx. 127	appx. 85	appx. 64	appx. 51
24"	± 609 mm	appx. 305	appx. 152	appx. 102	appx. 76	appx. 61

Millimeters

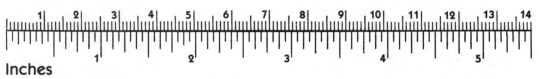

Inches

Bead and Cabochon Sizes

With few exceptions, beads and cabochons are measured by millimeters.

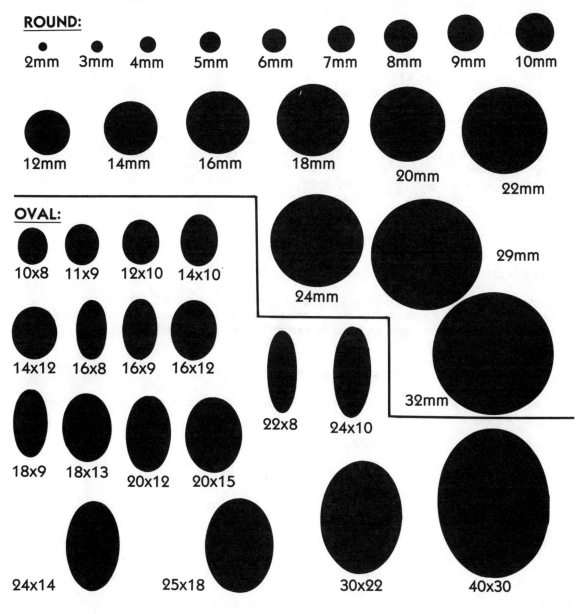

ROUND:

2mm   3mm   4mm   5mm   6mm   7mm   8mm   9mm   10mm

12mm   14mm   16mm   18mm   20mm   22mm

29mm

24mm

32mm

OVAL:

10x8   11x9   12x10   14x10

14x12   16x8   16x9   16x12

18x9   18x13   20x12   20x15

22x8   24x10

24x14   25x18   30x22   40x30

As if all that isn't enough, many beads are sold by the gram. You may be quoted a price per gram that seems SO inexpensive, but a gram is such a small unit that when it totals up, it's a bit of a shock! Here's some metric weight conversions:

METRIC		U.S. SYSTEM (AVOIRDUPOIS)	
METRIC TON:	1,000 kilograms (kg)	**"SHORT" TON:**	2,000 pounds (lbs.)
KILOGRAM:	2.2 pounds (lbs.)	**POUND:**	16 ounces (oz.)
	35.27 ounces		453.49 grams
GRAM:	.035 ounces	**OUNCE:**	28.35 grams
	15.43 grains		437.5 grains
	5 metric carats (ct)		141.75 carats (ct)

There's also TROY WEIGHT, which is not used very often. I didn't put this into the above table, lest it get too confusing. A POUND TROY is 12 ounces, 373.24 grams, 0.373 kilograms; an OUNCE TROY is 1.09 ounces avoir.(U.S. system), 31.11 grams, 155.51 carats; a PENNYWEIGHT is .0034 pounds avoir. (U.S. system), .054 ounce avoir., 1.55 grams, 7.77 carats; a GRAIN is 1 grain avoir., .065 gram, .32 carat, 64.8 milligrams.

Pretty confusing, huh!

Beads are sold by weight, by the strand, or by quantity.

The most common weight of beads is a kilogram, or ½ kilogram. Sometimes ounces or grams are used. Beware silver beads priced by the gram; sometimes pitch is inside to give 100% silver strength, and you're paying the same price per weight for the pitch as you are for silver.

Most strands are 16"; Half-strands are 8".

When buying in quantity, you will hear "gross" (144 pieces, or 12 dozen), or mass (1200 pieces, or 100 dozen).

Seed and Bugle Beads

Very small beads are called seedbeads. These come in different sizes and finishes, and require smaller, finer needles and thread. Traditionally, they are "woven" into intricate designs. Bead artists will tell you that they either LOVE seedbeads or HATE them. At times, they can be frustrating, but once you've worked with them, you will marvel at their beauty.

Seedbeads are measured by a very unusual method. They're not sized like other beads; sizing is based on the size of the rods used for making the glass beads (measured in increments called "aughts", which are roughly equivalent to ½ centimeter. Aught means 0). The smaller the number, the larger the bead. Thus, 11/0 is smaller than 7/0. What this really means is 11x0, versus 7x0 (sort of on a negative scale). Like in electronics, higher multiples of aught are actually smaller than lower multiples of aught. Pretty confusing, huh? To further complicate matters, each country that produces these beads has a different sizing system, so a Czech 11/0 may differ slightly from a Japanese 11/0. The chart on the right is based on Czech sizing.

BUGLE BEADS:

Bugle beads are measured by their lengths. Most bugle beads are made to be compatible with a size 11/0 seedbead's diameter. Sometimes you will find other diameters in bugle beads, but this is considered unusual. Longer bugle beads are measured by millimeters, shorter ones by the table below. They can be straight, or twisted. They come in many finishes. The most common sizes are:

| ½ | 1 | 2 | 3 | 4 | 5 |

	16/0
	15/0
	14/0
	13/0
	12/0
	11/0
	10/0
	9/0
	8/0
	7/0
	6/0
	5/0
	4/0
	3/0
	2/0
	1/0

Some descriptions you may hear about seedbeads and bugle beads are:

BUGLE BEADS - Long, tube shaped beads available in several lengths (see above).

CARNIVAL GLASS - brightly colored clear glass beads, made in the early part of the century.

CEYLON - Also called "pearl", has a glossy, creamy ("pearlized") finish.

CHALKWHITE - Dull finish, white opaque seedbeads.

CHARLOTTE BEAD - Traditionally used in Native American beadwork, a size 13/0 opaque seed bead that is cut and faceted like crystal. (very difficult to find).

"E" BEAD - A size 6/0 bead.

FROST - Frosted finish

HEXAGON-CUT - Bead cut with 6 sides; reflects light.

INDIAN BEAD - An opaque "pony" bead.

IRIS - Transluscent, glossy appearance.

LINED - Color inside a bead with a clear or tinted surface outside (sometimes not too colorfast)

LUSTRE - Has a very glassy, "bright" quality

METALLIC - Has a metallic finish, available in traditional metal colors (gold, bronze, silver), and also other bright colors.

OPAQUE LUSTRE - Glossy, deep color

OPAQUE DYED - Opaque, but with a muted, almost "watercolor" look; sometimes not completely colorfast.

RAINBOW - Bright, clear, vivid colors (carnival glass)

ROCAILLE - Silver or gold lined, with square holes.

SILKY CUT - Satiny, silky finish. Also known as **"SATIN"**.

STEEL BEADS - Faceted seedbeads made of steel used for embellishing many items before the war (i.e., purses, hats, etc.)

THREE-CUT - Highly reflective bead, with three surfaces showing at one time. This really catches the light. Used often on clothing.

TILE CUT - A very squared cyllindrical bead that weaves well due to its uniformity (like a short bugle bead).

TRANSLUCENT - "French Opal"

TRANSPARENT - clear glass

TWO-CUT - Reflective bead, with two surfaces showing at one time.

WHITE HEART BEADS - Beads of a deep color on the outside with white "chalky" centers. Usually found with deep red coloring.

Bead & Stone Shapes/Cuts/Surfaces

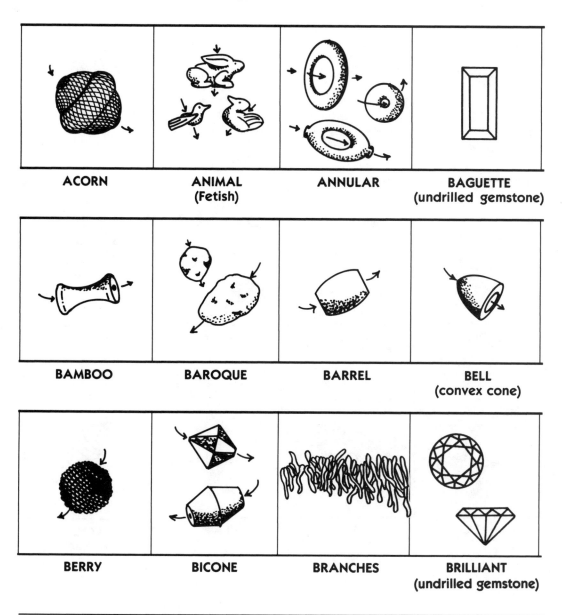

ACORN

ANIMAL
(Fetish)

ANNULAR

BAGUETTE
(undrilled gemstone)

BAMBOO

BAROQUE

BARREL

BELL
(convex cone)

BERRY

BICONE

BRANCHES

BRILLIANT
(undrilled gemstone)

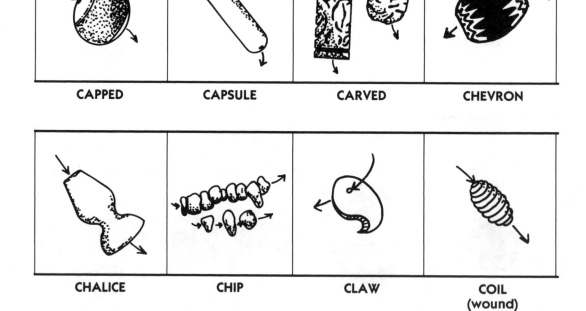

BULLET	BUTTON	CABOCHON (undrilled)	CAGE
CAPPED	CAPSULE	CARVED	CHEVRON
CHALICE	CHIP	CLAW	COIL (wound)

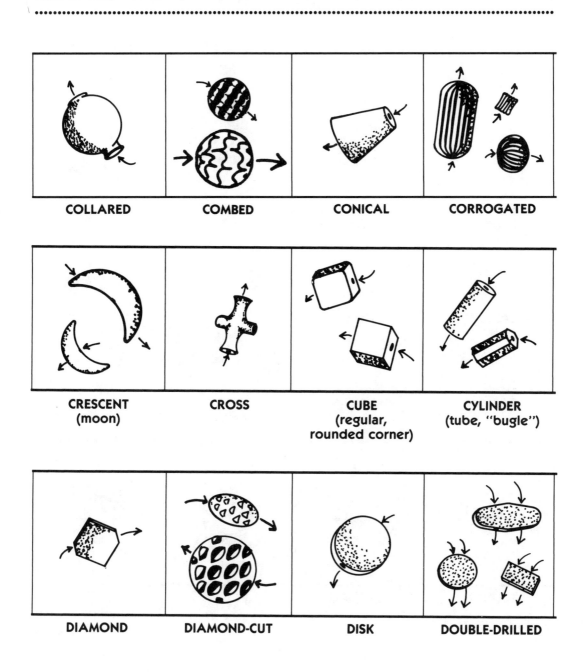

COLLARED	**COMBED**	**CONICAL**	**CORROGATED**
CRESCENT (moon)	**CROSS**	**CUBE** (regular, rounded corner)	**CYLINDER** (tube, "bugle")
DIAMOND	**DIAMOND-CUT**	**DISK**	**DOUBLE-DRILLED**

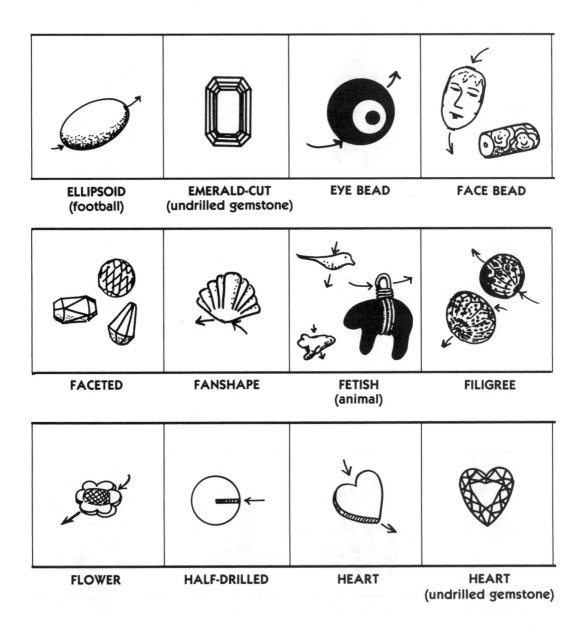

ELLIPSOID
(football)

EMERALD-CUT
(undrilled gemstone)

EYE BEAD

FACE BEAD

FACETED

FANSHAPE

FETISH
(animal)

FILIGREE

FLOWER

HALF-DRILLED

HEART

HEART
(undrilled gemstone)

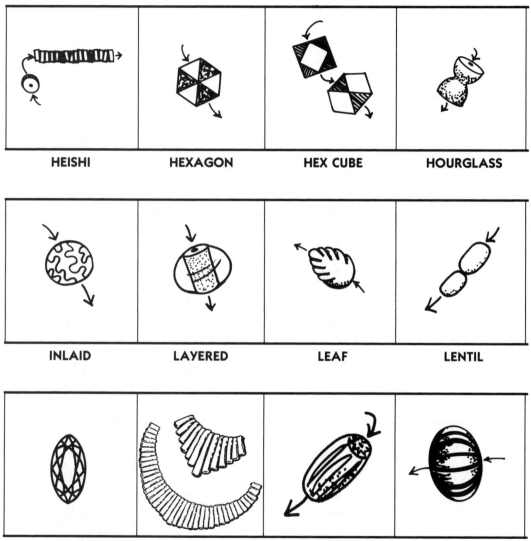

HEISHI	**HEXAGON**	**HEX CUBE**	**HOURGLASS**
INLAID	**LAYERED**	**LEAF**	**LENTIL**
MARQUISE (undrilled gemstone)	**MAXI (OR MINI)** **COLLAR**	**MELON**	**MELON-CUT**

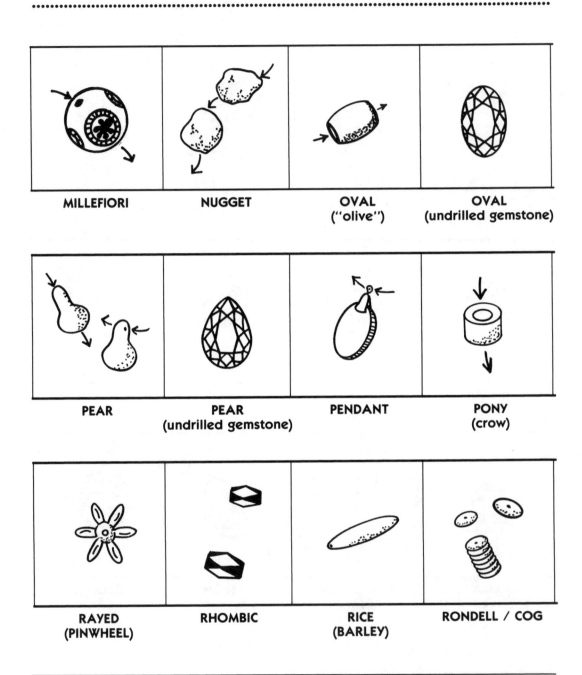

MILLEFIORI	NUGGET	OVAL ("olive")	OVAL (undrilled gemstone)
PEAR	PEAR (undrilled gemstone)	PENDANT	PONY (crow)
RAYED (PINWHEEL)	RHOMBIC	RICE (BARLEY)	RONDELL / COG

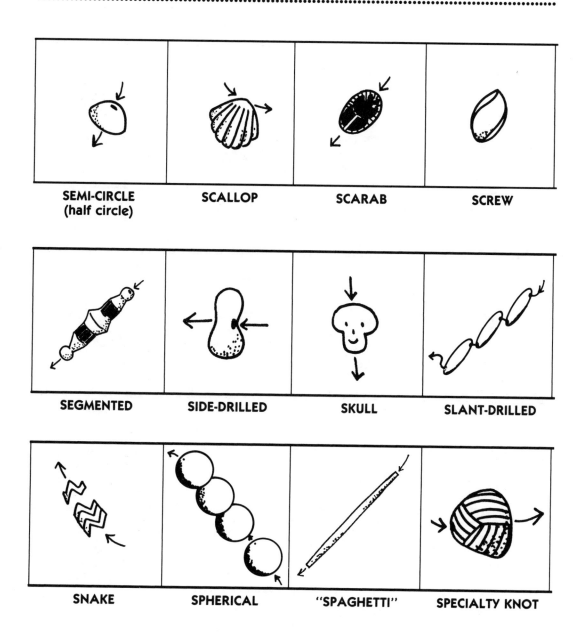

SEMI-CIRCLE (half circle)	**SCALLOP**	**SCARAB**	**SCREW**
SEGMENTED	**SIDE-DRILLED**	**SKULL**	**SLANT-DRILLED**
SNAKE	**SPHERICAL**	**"SPAGHETTI"**	**SPECIALTY KNOT**

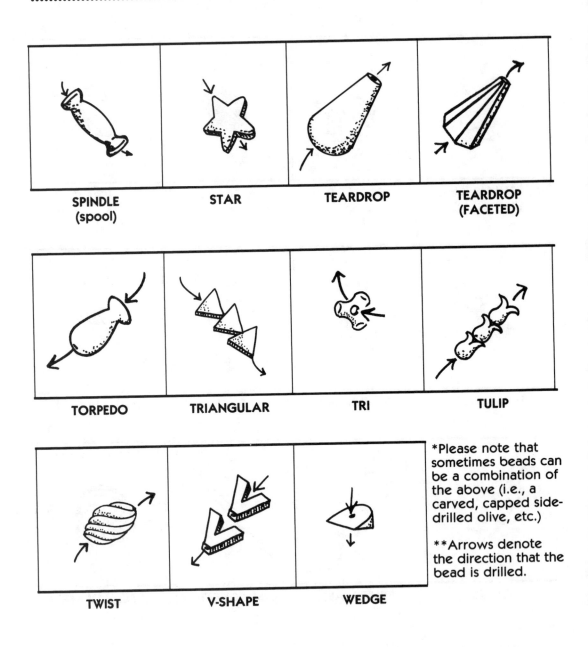

SPINDLE (spool)

STAR

TEARDROP

TEARDROP (FACETED)

TORPEDO

TRIANGULAR

TRI

TULIP

TWIST

V-SHAPE

WEDGE

*Please note that sometimes beads can be a combination of the above (i.e., a carved, capped side-drilled olive, etc.)

**Arrows denote the direction that the bead is drilled.

Types of Beads

AGATE — **Blue Lace,** icy blue; **Botswana,** earth tones; **Moss Agate,** green moss-like pattern. Member of chalcedony family.

AMAZONITE — light blue-green, member of the Feldspar family.

AMBER — not a true stone, this is a fossilized resin. Color ranges from bright yellow to deeper honey color to deep reddish brown (cherry amber). Amber floats, and holds an electric charge.

AMETHYST — colors range from deep purple to pale lavendar ("Cape Amethyst"). Gets its color from iron that is present. Member of the Quartz family.

AVENTURINE — green member of Quartz family, also known as "Indian Jade". Sometimes enhanced to other colors.

AZURITE — deep blue to lighter blue.

BERYL — **Aquamarine** blue-green, different from "Oriental Emerald", which it is not; **Emerald** green, very brittle; **Golden Beryl,** yellow; **Morganite,** purple, red, or pink.

BLOODSTONE — deep green with red flecks, also known as Heliotrope. A member of the Chalcedony family.

BONE — usually camel or bison bone, sometimes from other types of animals. Looks very much like ivory, but is much less expensive. Usually from India.

CARNELIAN — "Red Agate", shades of orange to deeper red; member of chalcedony family.

CHALCEDONY — blue to gray

CHRYSOPHASE — green to green-blue, member of chalcedony family.

CHRYSOBERYL — Alexandrite (artificial light makes the natural blue-green color look red or purple); Chrysoberyl (colors: brown, yellow, green, blue, and blue-green); Cymophane (also called "Cat's Eye"); usually cut into cabochons to show off cat's eye effect.

CINNABAR — (mercury sulfide) Rust red, used as vermillion.

CITRINE — yellow member of the Quartz family.

COPPER — a soft metal; reddish, but can tarnish to black; said to draw moisture, not attract it.

CORAL — not a true stone, but formed from the skeletal remains of underwater animals.

DIAMONDS — colors: Colorless, "Fancies" (Slight to deep coloration), Black Diamonds

FLUORITE — colors range from purple streaked with blue, yellow, brown, white and red, to deep blue. Sometimes resembles amethyst (sometimes called "Fool's Amethyst").

GARNET — Almadine (warm red to brown), sometimes called "California Ruby"; **Andradite**, wine red, green, yellow, brown, black; **Grossular**, white, yellow, pink, green (called "African Jade"), colorless, brown); **Pyrope** (deep red); **Rhodolite** (red); **Spessartine** (warm red to brown)

GLASS — manmade in various places around the world with regional characteristics; available in every color and finish imaginable; sometimes given a coating (i.e., "Aurora Borealis"); sometimes made to resemble gemstones when ground and made into paste form (rhinestones).

GOLD — very soft metal; pure gold is 24K, also available in smaller concentrations of 18K, 14K, and 10K.

GOLDSTONE — manmade glass with copper or other metals in tiny concentrations to reflect; looks like Sunstone, and comes in gold or blue tones.

HEMATITE — metallic, shiny black to candy-apple red; leaves red mark when scratched; used as "red ochre" in powdered form for paints; sometimes called "Alaska Diamond". The synthetic version of Hematite is called "Hematine".

HOWLITE — white with gray to black veining; in dyed form, used as a low-cost substitute for lapiz or turquoise.

IOLITE — Deep sapphire-blue color, also looks like blue Tourmaline. Sometimes called "Water Sapphire" or "Lynx Sapphire", but actually not a sapphire at all.

IVORY — from the tusks of elephants and walruses; currently there is a ban on new ivory (due to cruel harvesting practices).

JADE — Jadeite (most famous is green, but also comes in lavender, white, yellow, red); **Nephrite** is also called "Jade", but is usually green to creamy white. Jadeite is rarer and more expensive.

JASPER — Landscape (or Picture) Jasper (resembles landscape scene); **Red Jasper** ("Rust Jasper"); **Reptile (Leopard Skin)**, design like a reptile's skin.

JET — black, organically resulting from the decomposition of driftwood, a form of coal. Sometimes called "Black Amber".

LABRADORITE — gray, green, blue, red, multicolor; sometimes irridescent like opals. A member of the Feldspar family.

LAZURITE — Lapiz Lazuli (vivid blue with pyrite veining that resembles gold)

MAGNETITE (LODESTONE) — magnetic black iron oxide.

MALACHITE — dark green streaked with lighter green (opaque) — very rich looking color.

MARCASITE — pale yellow, gray, black; very similiar to **PYRITE**, but stronger and more stable. Usually used as faceted stones set in sterling.

MOONSTONE — milky white to beige-orange, a member of the Feldspar family.

OBSIDIAN — volcanic (resulting from lava that cooled too quickly). Varieties include: **Apache Tears** (transparent to translucent black/brown); **Mahogany** (opaque black with brown streaks); **Snowflake Obsidian** (opaque black with white specks and streaks) sometimes called "Flower Obsidian"

OLIVINE — **Peridot** (from yellow green to deep green with olive tones); sometimes called "The Evening Emerald", but not the same as "Peridot of Brazil" or "Peridot of Ceylon", which are both tourmalines.

ONYX — orange to milky white, bands run in straight lines, vs. agate that has angled, curved coloration.

OPAL — **Black Opal** (black, dark blue, dark green, gray); **Fire Opal** (orange-yellow to red to multi-color); **White Opal** (white or light color)

PEARL — when a foreign object gets into an oyster, the oyster's immune system coats it with "nacre" (calcium carbonate), which thickens as time progresses. See section on "How to Know What You're Buying" for more information on pearls and their care.

PLATINUM — very white to metallic gray, does not tarnish.

PYRITE — yellowish to greenish black; commonly called "Fool's Gold"; sometimes confused with marcasite, which it is not.

QUARTZ — **Milky Quartz** (milky white); **Rock Crystal** (clear); **Rose Quartz** (pink) gets it color from titanium that is present; **Rutilated Quartz** (clear with black and gray "needles" running throughout); **Smoky Quartz** (gray); gets its color from natural radiation that is present

RHODOCHROSITE — red to pink, with circular bands of different shades of the same colors.

RHODONITE — rose-colored, but also found in red and brown-red with some black veins.

RUBY — (red), value ranges from moderate (pink) to high (deep, clear red). Member of the Corundum family (Sapphire and Emery (as in emery boards) are other two members).

SAPPHIRE — (deep blue) — can be cut to show off natural beauty of stone ("Star Sapphire").

SERPENTINE — color ranges from red to white to green (sometimes called "Korea Jade"); very similiar to Nephrite.

SHELL — **Mother-of-Pearl** (this name makes perfect sense when you think about it); **Cat's Eye** (brown to green), used as cabochons; **Cowrie Shell,** from a mollusk.

SILVER — silvery white, but tarnishes to brown or black, very soft; available in different concentrations; sterling is designated with the marking "925" (this means 92.5% silver).

SOAPSTONE — actually steatite (white to green); very soft stone.

SODALITE — blue is best known, but also in gray, white, and green.

SPINELS — color ranges include purple, blue, and red; Used as a less-expensive substitute for sapphires and rubies.

SUNSTONE — multi-color to white to gray to bluish (flecked with hematite)

TIGER EYE — brown, irridescence caused by suspended fibers of asbestos; sometimes called "Hawk's Eye"

TOPAZ — **Blue Topaz** sometimes heat or humidity will deepen the color, but this usually fades back to normal; **Dark Red ("Hyacinth")** heat treating this creates a lighter red variety; also seen as **Green Topaz, Yellow Topaz,** and **Golden Brown Topaz.**

TOURMALINE — **Dravite** (orange to brown); **Indiocolite** (blue); **Rubellite** (red); **Watermelon** (most famous — green to pink)

TURQUOISE — blue, blue-green, warm green

VESUVIANITE (Idocrase) — **"California Jade"** (Translucent; green/gray with green streaks — NOT related to true jade)

ZIRCON — **Blue Zircon,** highest value; **Hyacinth or Jacinth,** red; **Jargoon,** clear or gray; Also found in brown, blue, green, purple. Sometimes heat-treated to bring out color, but effect doesn't last — fades in light over a period of time.

THE BEST LITTLE BEADING BOOK

How to Know What You're Buying

I t's very easy to be mistaken when you're buying beads. Even the most honest supplier can inadvertently misidentify his wares. There are, however, a few clues that can help you. Your best asset is your knowledge; visit as many dealers and gem shows as is possible until you get a feel for what different beads look like.

The most common errors are:

- **Sodalite being identified as lapiz**
  Lapiz is a richer, more royal blue with metallic veining, while sodalite is a grayer steel-blue with white veining.

- **Dyed howlite being passed off as turquoise or lapiz.**
  The real stuff is less uniform in color; the dyed stuff is too uniform. Also, howlite does not have the metallic veining of lapiz, or the variation or depth of real turquoise.

- **Sometimes aventurine is mistaken for jade.**
  Aventurine has little "lines" of a slightly deeper green that are almost irridescent.

- **Plastic is mistaken for amber.**
  Some plastics are very good, and it is difficult to tell the difference. Amber holds an electric charge. If you rub it on your arm, the little hairs should stand up from static electricity. Plastic does not hold this charge.

- **Plastic is mistaken for glass.**
  A dead giveaway is if the bead has seams with a lot of extra material stuck to it (seams) — glass doesn't. Also, check the weight (more on this later).

- **Garnets are died on the inside to a deeper, richer color.**
  See if the string has picked up the color.

- **Phony pearls.**
  Some people like to rub pearls on their teeth — real pearls feel gritty, false pearls are smooth (Personally, I'm not fond of testing merchandise on dental work). Some false pearls are called "Laguna Pearls". Once you've seen some pearls, the differences should become quite evident.

- **Marcasite is not always as it's marked.**
  Sometimes it's really hematite, sometimes pyrite, sometimes God-knows-what. If it's set in sterling silver, you stand a better chance of getting the real thing.

- **Hematine is a synthetic version of Hematite.**
  Usually priced at far less, its one real disadvantage is that it scratches so easily.

The most common enhancing techniques (that's what it's called — "enhancing") employ artificial methods to color the beads. The ones used most are heat, radiation, and dyes.

• **Heat** is used to deepen, lighten , or totally change the color. Amethysts can be heated to resemble citrine or topaz; aquamarine can be heated to deepen the color.

• **Radiation** is used to deepen the color, i.e., the blue of topaz.

• **Using Dyes** — as already mentioned: lapiz, howlite, and garnets, in addition to black onyx (which does not occur naturally in nature, and is actually dyed chalcedony), jade (from deepening the color to totally changing it), lapiz (to deepen the color and simulate a more expensive piece), carnelian, and just about any other stone. The best test is a cotton swab with a dab of alcohol (some say de-natured alcohol, but any kind will do). If the color comes off, it's dyed.

My own personal methods of testing are color, temperature, pitch, and weight.

Color — If the color is too uniform or looks funny, I question it. You shouldn't pay as much for dyed stones as those that are naturally colored.

Temperature — If the temperature is cooler than it should be, or not as cool (plastic is warm, glass is cooler, and, depending on density, stones should be the coolest).

Pitch — the sound it makes when gently rapped on a table. Does it "thunk" with a heavy, dense sound (real stone); a higher pitch (glass); or the empty high pitch of plastic?

Weight — plastic, the least dense, is very light (but so is amber, which can be confusing). Glass is usually heavier, and, again depending on density, real stone beads should be even heavier. Hematite is about the heaviest I've found.

Again, the best thing you can do is get familiar with what's out there and develop your own system.

Once you have bought pearls, you must be careful not to scratch them (that's one reason to knot your thread between them in necklaces). It's best to keep them clean. Use a **safe** pearl cleaner or gentle dish washing detergent (white or clear, not green or colored — the pearl will pick up the color). Wipe them off after you have worn them, and be careful not to get hairspray or perfume on them (which will dull or damage the coating). Also, keep them away from sharp objects — they wound easily.

I know a lady who wanted to dye her pearls. She soaked them in tea and left them overnight. Unfortunately, they turned to mush by morning!

●●●

Findings

●●●

A finding is anything that is not a bead. This includes clasps, earwires, knot covers, etc. It's very confusing when you are trying to design a piece and you're not sure what you need. The following pages feature findings of all kinds.

EARRING FINDINGS — PIERCED

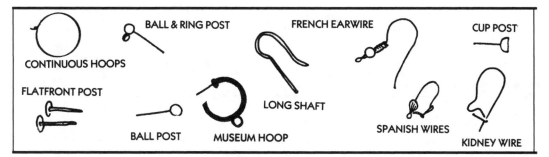

EARRING FINDINGS — UNPIERCED

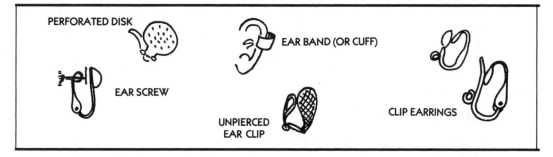

EARRING FINDINGS — MISC.

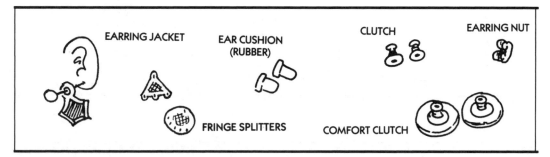

Findings

NECKLACE FINDINGS — CLASPS

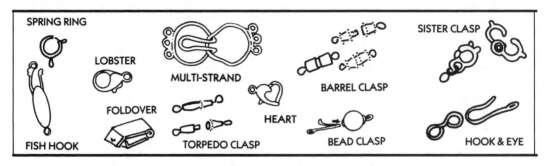

SPRING RING

LOBSTER

MULTI-STRAND

FOLDOVER

FISH HOOK

TORPEDO CLASP

HEART

BARREL CLASP

BEAD CLASP

SISTER CLASP

HOOK & EYE

NECKLACE FINDINGS — GENERAL

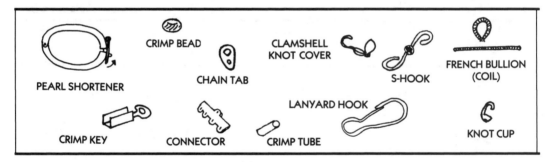

CRIMP BEAD

CLAMSHELL KNOT COVER

S-HOOK

FRENCH BULLION (COIL)

PEARL SHORTENER

CHAIN TAB

LANYARD HOOK

CRIMP KEY

CONNECTOR

CRIMP TUBE

KNOT CUP

MISCELLANEOUS FINDINGS

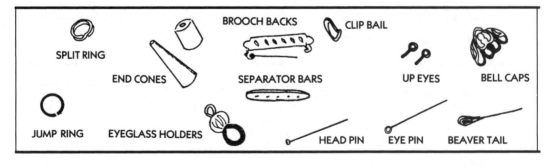

BROOCH BACKS

CLIP BAIL

SPLIT RING

END CONES

SEPARATOR BARS

UP EYES

BELL CAPS

JUMP RING

EYEGLASS HOLDERS

HEAD PIN

EYE PIN

BEAVER TAIL

Chain Shapes / Configurations

Using chain in your jewelry is a great way to enhance the design and give a variety of shapes. The problem is, most people don't stop and think about what kind of chain they want to use . . . believe it or not, there are dozens! Some work for jewelry, but some have such small, difficult links, that they're just not usable.

A SUGGESTION: the best ones have links that are easy to thread (Charm, Figure Eight, Curb, etc.). The worst ones have almost invisible definitions between links (Herring, Wheat, Scroll, etc.).

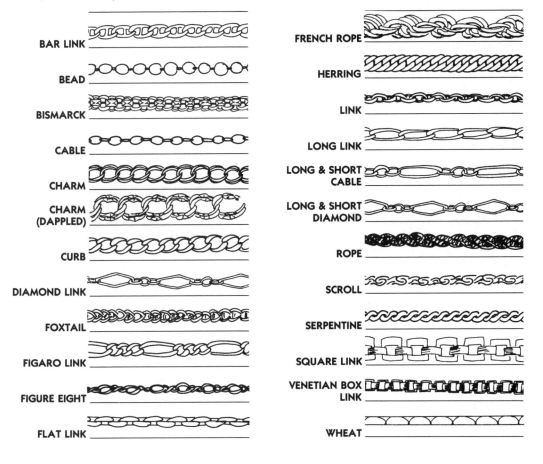

BAR LINK

BEAD

BISMARCK

CABLE

CHARM

CHARM (DAPPLED)

CURB

DIAMOND LINK

FOXTAIL

FIGARO LINK

FIGURE EIGHT

FLAT LINK

FRENCH ROPE

HERRING

LINK

LONG LINK

LONG & SHORT CABLE

LONG & SHORT DIAMOND

ROPE

SCROLL

SERPENTINE

SQUARE LINK

VENETIAN BOX LINK

WHEAT

Stringing Media

When undertaking a necklace, the first question asked is always: "What do I string it on?" There are ten zillion types of thread, cord, nylon, silk and wire out there. To complicate things further, they each come in a dozen sizes.

How do you know what size (weight) you need? CALIBRATE YOUR STRINGING MEDIUM TO THE SIZE OF THE HOLE IN YOUR BEADS. Your goal is to fill up the hole with the thickest possible thread (or whatever), to reduce the friction that will lead to the eventual breaking of your jewelry.

Certain beads have very large holes (garnets) or very small holes (hematite) that have no proportional relationship to the size of the bead. Always bring a bead from your intended necklace when purchasing your stringing supplies.

I would love to be able to tell you to buy Brand X in X weight, but unfortunately, your choice of supplies may be limited where you live. I've mentioned some brand names, but I think it is of more value to tell you the type of material you're looking for. Then, if you can't find Brand X, at least you'll know if Brand Y does the trick.

SILK THREAD ON SPOOLS

Traditionally used with real pearls, it also works well with most semi-precious or glass beads. It's ended with knot cups or covers, French coil, or knotted under end caps or inside beads. It is knotable (this is what you use to knot between beads). The colors will thrill you: almost any color you can think of! It's sized like shoe sizes: 00, 0, A, B, C, D, E, F, FF, FFF (with AA the thinnest, and FFF the heaviest). It's used with twisted wire needles. The appearance is soft and silky, with a beautiful sheen (my Mom uses this for counted cross-stitch). The advantage to buying this on a cone (or spool) is that you have a larger amount to work with at one time. Some projects require lots of this thread (like Needleweaving), and purchasing smaller amounts will put you at a disadvantage. The spool is very convenient. Manufacturers include: Gudebrod, Rice, Belding Corticelli. The best general purpose weight for most semi-precious beads is "F".

SILK THREAD ON CARDS

These are convenient if you only want to do one or two necklaces. They have the needles already attached, and the thread is already doubled on the card. Not practical if you do a lot of beadwork. The needles are not reusable.

NYLON BEAD CORD

Very similiar to silk in appearance and weight, except it's a little stiffer, and sometimes seems to be a little stronger. You can knot this like silk. It comes in the same weights (same calibration system) as silk. It's almost interchangeable with silk, although purists will tell you they like silk better. Again, it's available on both spools and cards. I find spools more practical.

NYMO

A nylon thread similar in consistency to dental floss, but definitely better. I find this works best for fresh water pearls, seed bead necklaces, beadweaving, etc. (NOT INTENDED FOR HEAVY BEADS!) It has a totally different calibration system than silk, and is very limited in colors. Available usually in white, black, and brown, rarely is it available in colors (You can easily color this with a permanent marking pen). This seems to come in two different measurements: One way uses "0's" (000, 00, 0, with 0 the thickest), and A, B, C, D, E, F, G (G is the thickest). Nymo comes with a waxed finish, except "A", which is very thin and breaks easily. I don't like working with A — it's like trying to sew with a cobweb. You need to strengthen it by waxing it with bee's wax. I prefer B, 0 or 00 for weaving seedbeads in earrings, and D or F for freshwater pearls or seedbead necklaces. This can be ended with French coil or knot cups/covers; it can also be used for bead loom work. It's usually available on little bobbins or slightly larger spools.

WAXED LINEN

A heavy upholstery cord that's used for heavier projects. It's a little rough on the hands to use, but it's STRONG! It seems to only come in one weight, but many, many colors.

TIGER TAIL

This is the nickname for a nylon-coated wire cable. It's used for heavy or sharp beads (i.e., crystal that might cut silk). Used in conjunction with crimp beads, which have little "teeth" inside (See section on stringing). Some people like to use it for glass or semi-precious, although, being a wire, it won't drape as nicely as silk or nylon does. It's great for bracelets and anklets, as it can withstand lots of movement without breaking. It's never used with pearls or very light weight beads, because being a wire, it will take on a life of its own. It comes in sizes .012, .015, .018, .020, and .024, with .012 the thinnest, and .024 the heaviest. NEVER knot the tiger tail itself, as it is a wire and it will kink and break!

COTTON EMBROIDERY FLOSS

Lacks the sheen of silk, but ok to use sometimes for temporary knotting or stringing. It's great for kids to practice with. It is so darn inexpensive, and the colors are great (even varigated). If you buy one skein, you do have all of the weights, as you can split the threads to make a variety of thicknesses. You can make a great special effect by knotting a varigated thread. Each knot is a different color, and it's great fun. Just remember — cotton's not meant to be forever, as it will stretch, and eventually, it rots.

"RAT TAIL / MOUSE TAIL" SATIN CORDING

"Rat Tail" is 2mm thick, "Mouse Tail" is 1mm thick. It's great for stringing larger beads or carved pieces (used for Chinese knotting). Found in fabric stores, it's usually bought by the foot or yard. The colors are wonderful. A similiar version is made of corduroy and used for upholstery.

LEATHER OR SUEDE CORD

Leather is available in a variety of colors and weights, from ½mm to 1mm to 2mm. It knots nicely, and surfers and swimmers like the leather because they can wear it into the ocean and it will last for awhile (but it will eventually break down because of the salt water).

MISCELLANEOUS STRINGING MEDIA

There's a use for everything, right? Bedspread crochet cotton and pearlized polished cotton can be used for certain projects, although they have the same drawbacks as embroidery floss.

When in doubt, test for strength (can you break it easily?) and coarseness (does it hurt your fingers to work with it?) and colorfastness (does it fade badly?). Also, don't rule out yarns, ultra-suede scraps, or bits of fabric.

NEVER USE . . .

• **DENTAL FLOSS** — It's biodegradable and not meant to last. Also, the flavored versions attract ants.

• **NYLON FILAMENT** (Used for fishing) — It melts; it cracks; it ages. It won't last!

Needles

Nothing is worse than not having the right needle for your projects. If the needle is too big, it won't go through your beads. If it's too small, you can't thread it. These are the needles you'll use the most for bead work:

TWISTED WIRE
Used for knotting pearls. Very fragile; usually not reusable. Has a collapsing eye that helps grip the thread.

ENGLISH BEADING NEEDLES
The smaller the needle, the larger the number. Calibrated to work with seed beads; A #10 needle works with a #10 seed bead.

SHARPS
Great for beading on leather; Fairly fine with small round eyes; good and strong. Comes in different sizes.

TAPISTRY
Has a large eye with a blunt point. Good with very large beads. A good needle for children to use.

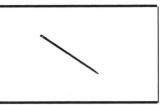

EMBROIDERY
Like a needlepoint needle, easy to thread (eyes are long). Usually thicker, works with large beads.

BETWEENS
Used for quilting, it's shorter than a SHARPS, and finer. Works with leather & smaller beads.

DARNING
Long, sharp needle with long eye. Easy to thread, used for weaving, or with larger beads.

FLOSSING NEEDLES
Not really a needle, its primary use is for dental work. Nice large eye that's easy to thread; very sturdy & reusable.

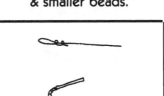

HOMEMADE NEEDLES
Using a 2" length of 28 gauge wire, fold over & twist. OR, use cement on end of thread to stiffen & become a self-needle.

Pliers

Having the right tool is half the job when it comes to jewelry-making. Pliers are one of your most important tools. Use them for gripping, turning, bending wire, closing loops . . . you name it! Almost every project in this book needs pliers of one kind or another.

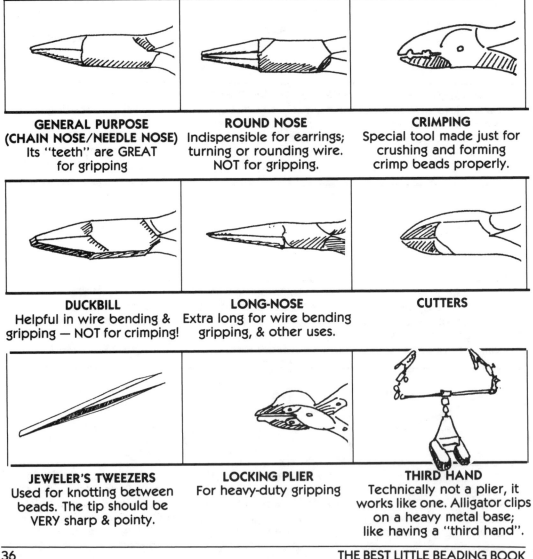

**GENERAL PURPOSE
(CHAIN NOSE/NEEDLE NOSE)**
Its "teeth" are GREAT
for gripping

ROUND NOSE
Indispensible for earrings;
turning or rounding wire.
NOT for gripping.

CRIMPING
Special tool made just for
crushing and forming
crimp beads properly.

DUCKBILL
Helpful in wire bending &
gripping — NOT for crimping!

LONG-NOSE
Extra long for wire bending
gripping, & other uses.

CUTTERS

JEWELER'S TWEEZERS
Used for knotting between
beads. The tip should be
VERY sharp & pointy.

LOCKING PLIER
For heavy-duty gripping

THIRD HAND
Technically not a plier, it
works like one. Alligator clips
on a heavy metal base;
like having a "third hand".

THE BEST LITTLE BEADING BOOK

Anatomy of a Bead Box

Now that you know about needles, pliers, threads, etc., what else should you include in your bead box?

NEEDLE FILES
For smoothing out
rough beads

BABY WIPES
For cleaning most beads
in a safe way

NAIL CLIPPERS
For trimming tiger tail

SMALL SPOONS
Whether your nails are long
or short, you'll be glad to
have these for scooping
beads.

SCOTCH TAPE
For gripping

FUNNELS
For helping cleanup
seedbeads

A BEAD BOARD
Helps with designing

FILM CANS
For storing small beads.

VITAMIN CONTAINERS
For keeping little findings
and seedbeads.

Glues / Cements

Glue vs. Cement: The debates continue! Both have very unique properties. How do you know when it's appropriate to use either? The wrong adhesive can be deadly if it dissolves your finding. I've not used brand names because different products are available in different areas. Using the descriptions given, you should have no problem finding suitable products to work with.

WHITE CRAFTERS' GLUE

There are several great brands on the market. What distinguishes a "crafters' glue" from a regular white glue is that white glue tends to be thinner. In a pinch, they're almost interchangable.

Glue is non-invasive — it doesn't soak in, it sits on top of what you're adhering. With non-porous surfaces, this is usually okay. With porous surfaces, you may want a little stronger "bite".

Glues are usually white or cream-colored. They are usually water-soluable, and excess can be removed easily with a fingernail. Sometimes, the bond doesn't seem very permanent.

The good thing is, that if you're trying to bond a plastic cabochon, glue won't eat up the backing the way that a cement will.

WATCH MAKER'S CEMENT

Watch Makers' Cement is different from regular cement because the "grain" of it seems smaller — it seems to soak in better for fine work. Being a cement, it does penetrate what it is bonding. It's ideal for cementing the knots in your threads when you do beadwork, although it's NOT strong enough for a heavy-duty metal to bead bond. It has a tiny little applicator tip, so it doesn't glop everywhere when you use it. This seems to work well with most rhinestones (it doesn't dissolve the backs). It makes a bond that is rigid. Drying time is about 5 minutes.

CRAFTERS' CEMENT

This is the cement you find in craft stores. The applicators are usually not really fine, and sometimes you need to apply (sparingly) with a toothpick. If it dries with a lot of excess, you will see it and not be able to remove it. This has more "bite" than the previous cement, and has been known to dissolve the backings off of rhinestones. It will give you a nice, industrial strength bond, and you can use it for adhere beads to findings, metal-to-metal, etc. Drying times differ from brand to brand, from 5 minutes to 24 hours, depending on your use. The thicker the cemented area, the longer it will take to dry.

EPOXY

This stuff is very invasive! It will bond your jewelry, you, and the table together on contact! It's best to have epoxy remover on hand when you use this (I could tell you a gruesome story about an overeager woman who epoxied an earring to her ear, but I won't). Use it will semi-precious stones. Epoxy will eat the backings off of rhinestones, and (sometimes) the plating off of findings. It's makes a VERY permanent bond. Use it sparingly, it bonds instantly.

SILICONE GLUE

Found in hardware or plumbing departments, it "beads up" and makes a bond with anything, it's very gloppy. Resembles hot glue-gun glueing, but cool, so can be used where heat could be a problem. Used in the 1970's for "3-D" picture glueing. It's very flexible, and "breathes". Great for making "glitzy" earrings and brooches. Takes about a day to dry.

HOT GLUE GUN

My favorite is the mini-glue gun, because it's much easier to handle. Don't even **think** about getting one without a trigger (saves you from minor burns). The glue cartridges are amazingly inexpensive. The biggest drawback is that you must be very careful on meltable surfaces. (Also, use sparingly . . . it glops). The low-heat ones are of no use — if you leave what you glued in a hot car, it will come apart. It dries quickly, as it cools.

OTHER ADHESIVES

• In a pinch, CLEAR NAIL POLISH will work for cementing knots, although it's not made to be permanent.
• SPRAY ADHESIVES are quick and wonderful, although they can be a pit messy if the overspray gets on furniture. Use for adhering paper or leather.
• MODEL CEMENT is very much like epoxy, and can be used in a pinch to hold findings together. Takes a long time to dry.
• There are special METAL GLUES designed for glueing metals together. Some of these bond with heat or ultraviolet light. This is a little more complex process.

As always, common sense should prevail. Use your adhesives in a smart way, with good ventilation.

Paints and Dyes

Sometimes you may want to change or enhance the color of your thread, wooden beads, or leather.

PERMANENT MARKERS

While some threads are available in many colors, others may be limited. The easiest way to get a good variety is to use a permanent marking pen. Being permanent, the color won't run. You can make your thread match your leather, beads, etc. The variety of colors is endless — graphic arts supply stores carry these markers in thousands of shades.

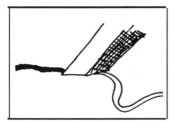

You can also use the permanent markers for coloring wooden beads (please see how-to section).

Markers come with different types of tips. "Chisel-point" tips work best for thread. When coloring your thread with a marker, it's best to draw the thread under the tip of the marker (see diagram). Fine-point tips work best for detail work (like coloring beads). Always let the marker dry before you try to use the thread you've just colored!

ACRYLICS

There are acrylic paints that are terrific for changing the color of wooden beads, or on leather or fabric. You can apply them with a brush, or thin them and use them in an airbrush (airbrush kits are fairly inexpensive, and can also be used for coloring ceramic beads, or other special effects). The "poor man's airbrush" is made by dipping an old toothbrush into a bowl of paint, then running your finger on top of the bristles to make a "spraying motion". Practice with just water first, or you may end up with a splattered outfit. Another fun effect is to take shaped cookie cutters and dip them into little bowls of paint. Apply them to fabric, and you'll have outlines to fill in (an easy stencil). Acrylics tend to "sit on top of fabric or leather", rather than soaking in. This tends to stiffen the fabric the somewhat. Acrylics can also be used as a glue to adhere rhinestones, etc. to clothing, and they're very quick to dry.

FABRIC PAINT

These come in self-applicator bottles, or accordian-squeezable tubes. This gives lots of control. Many of them puff up. Drizzle them on (Jackson Pollack-style) for earrings. They act as a glue if you drop beads and sequins into them while still wet. If you're beading clothing, these are great for adding definition to your designs.

DYES

Dyes tend to soak into, rather than sit on top of, whatever you use them on. Fabrics stay soft. Some dyes need to be set with heat. Some ultrasuedes are more porous than leather, so dyes can be a fun way of experimenting for special effects. You can "tie-dye", you can "batik", the list goes on and on! Just wear gloves with this one, because dyes also soak into SKIN!

MARBELIZING

If you're making paper earrings, or stiffened fabric earrings, marbelizing is a fun way to get some terrific special effects. Many companies make marbelizing kits, which include a suspension medium plus several colors of textile paint. It's very easy to do and the effects are quite elegant.

METAL PAINTS

Use the touch-up paint from the family car to color your findings! Your earrings can match your car! Seriously, it does work. Or, borrow your child's model car kit and use the paint in there on your findings. Also, there actually are several companies who now manufacture paints specifically made for coloring findings. They tend to be translucent, not opaque.

SPECIALTIES

Anything is adaptable . . . so experiment with food coloring, specialized textile paint, silk fabric paint, even tea or coffee. There's also inks, reactive dyes, watercolor paint, enamel paint, silkscreening paint, crayon and pastel (can be melted in with a hot iron — first color a design, then iron it). I've done this on brown paper supermarket bags, and ended up with something that really resembled fabric in texture. Remember to use a pressing cloth to protect your iron.

Design Fundamentals

There's more to making jewelry than just slapping together a bunch of pretty beads. There are aspects that you should be aware of when it comes to jewelry design.

Every piece that you create can be defined in the following ways:

FORMAT (Physical dimensions and appearance)
- Earrings
- Belt
- Necklace
- Etc.

STYLE (Design consideration and technique)
- Loomed
- Strung
- Woven
- Etc.
- Beaded

TONE (Degree of quality — materials)
- Plastic
- Pearls
- Semi-precious
- Etc.
- Glass

When designing a piece, it is best to first decide what your objectives are in regard to the above. If the piece is to look opulent, which techniques or materials will show that? If you are designing for a friend, what are their personal preferences? Considering these factors is essential to good jewelry design.

PRINCIPLES OF JEWELRY DESIGN

BALANCE (Arrangement of elements)

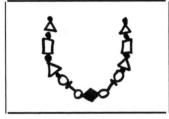
FORMAL BALANCE

INFORMAL BALANCE

MOSIAC COMPOSITION

FORMAL BALANCE is symmetrical — the left side of the necklace equals the right in a literal way. It denotes dignity, strength, and simplicity. If you're working with matched pearls, or all the same bead, or a symmetrical repeating pattern of beads, all of these are considered Formal Balance.

INFORMAL BALANCE is asymmetrical — the left and right sides appear balanced because of a number of elements of design. Informally balanced necklaces attract attention, and have an excitement to them.

MOSIAC COMPOSITION uses a lot of variety — it creates a lot of excitement by the mixtures of color. It's a great way to use up odds and ends of beads, as it look best when its "busy."

Composition is achieved through the use of color, texture, shape, movement, quantity, size, and proportion. Certain elements of design grab attention more than others:

Strong:	Weak:
• Dark	• Light
• Color	• Noncolor
• Unusual	• Usual
• Large	• Small
• Texture	• Smooth
• Glossy	• Dull
• Many	• Few

Proportion is a very strong factor. A large piece can overpower a small person, and a small, delicate piece can be lost on a larger person. When designing a necklace, you must take body size into consideration: where is the person's optical center? Also, take bosom size (of the intended wearer) into consideration when stringing necklaces: this can determine how a necklace hangs.

Repetition of elements can pull the necklace together; Opposition (Differences in materials/shapes/etc.) can create contrasts that are exciting. Create unity with your fill beads and accent pieces.

Standard necklace lengths are:
- **CHOKER** - at the throat, usually about 15 inches (depending on the individual's neck size).
- **PRINCESS** - 18 inches.
- **MATINEE** - 20 to 24 inches.
- **OPERA** - 28 to 30 inches.
- **LARIAT (OR ROPE)** - 45 inches or longer.

Sometimes your necklace will be all of one kind of bead (as in matched pearls). This is a very easy approach (yet not really artistically satisfying). If the only differing factor is the size of the beads, it is traditional to string them in graduated sizes, starting with your smallest in the back and the largest in center front.

However, if you hunger to let your artistic self be known, then the greatest joys come from creating with a mixed lot of beads.

When designing a necklace, you generally have a central focus piece, which could be one large accent piece, or a cluster of several smaller pieces. If these are positioned in the center of the necklace, then it is referred to as a **Center, Fetish,** or **Focus Piece** (see A below). If it hangs below the bead line (your thread), then it is referred to as a **Pendant** (see B below). If your Focus Piece is on the side, it is referred to as a **Station** (see C below).

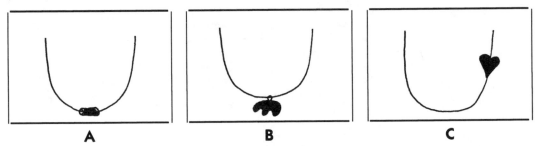

A   **B**   **C**

When choosing your accent piece, it should be fairly unique and stand out from the other beads. Using the values already mentioned, you can decide where you want your piece to be. Remember, large flat pieces work well as Stations, but tend to flip horizontally when used as a Center.

Using your bead board, you can lay out a design around this piece. The order of design is that your Focus Piece is considered your **Primary Piece**; your next beads are considered **Secondary**; the next beads are **Terciary**; and the final beads used are **Filler Beads** (see below). Unless you are a very rich person, it is recommended that you use your most expensive beads sparingly (as Primary or Secondary), and your less expensive beads where quantity is needed (Terciary or Filler).

The inches are marked on your bead board to help in the design process. For those who don't know what a bead board is, it's a sheet of vacuum-formed plastic or wood with a trough for your beads to lay in (please see section on tools). A nice easy way to design is to use these marks as a guide as to where to lay your beads (say, a blue bead every two inches; or a red bead every inch).

STEP ONE:
Lay your Primary
beads into position.

STEP TWO:
Now, add your
Secondary beads.

STEP THREE:
Add your Terciary beads,
and fill in the rest of the
necklace with Filler beads.

As you look at the bead board, you'll notice that the numbers run up both sides. Besides being a design tool, the bead board is also intended to tell you the finished length of the necklace. (If you take an 8" measurement from one side, and add that to the 8" measurement on the other, that tells you that this necklace will be 16" long).

Remember, it is quite unusual to put your fanciest and most expensive beads at the back of the necklace. Most people's hair or collars cover them up. Unless your necklace is a continuous design with no clasp, keep your fancies down toward the front. Sometimes it's deceptive as to where a bead will fall. You design it to show, but when you're done, it's too far back and no one sees it. Practice will remedy this. For the most part, it's best to put your inexpensive filler beads toward the back.

Multi-strand necklaces are very popular. There are several types of these.

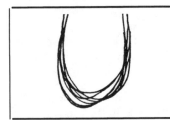

UNIFORM LENGTH
All strands are the same length, and can be twisted together.

GRADUATED LENGTH
A variety of lengths, used to create fullness. (works best with several strands).

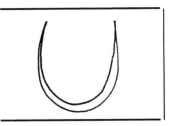

PARISIAN LOOP
Usually two strands, with 1" - 3" difference in length between them.

Using the same principle as that for a single strand, take it one step further to add additional strands. A multi-strand necklace is usually done in the mosiac style, but you can also make them symmetrical or asymmetrical.

With many multistrand necklaces, you do not want your accent beads to all fall in exactly the same place on each strand. It's best to stagger them, to give a fuller look.

Certain multistrand necklaces are very precise and need to be mapped out exactly how you want the design. One bead could throw the whole thing off. These require some thought, and you may want to work with graph paper and completely map out the design before you begin.

Please see the section on how-tos — there are several multi-strand necklaces.

Basics For Good Earring Design

There are several factors to take into consideration when designing earrings.

• Obviously, the most important is whether the person who wears them has pierced ears. Nowadays, most people do, but when you come across someone without pierced ears, it can pose a problem regarding your findings.

• For most earring designs it doesn't matter if they are on either pierced or unpierced findings; however, if someone who has unpierced ears wants a shorter look in an earring, it does rule out posts. For pierced ears, there is a variety of findings, ranging from posts to very long earwires.

• When designing, you should take into account several factors: if the intended wearer has long hair, sometimes earrings are a little lost and go unnoticed. A lot of women with short hair like spectacular earrings, because their ears are so visible. Many beauty salons sell earrings, because after a dramatic haircut many women look for new earrings to go with their new look.

• How long is the person's neck? People with short necks don't like long earrings.

• How heavy is the earring? Does it pull and drag on the ear?

• Remember to make your earrings mirror images (either the design faces in, or out). It looks a bit odd when both earrings are facing the same way (this can be a bit tricky when you're buying charms and they only come in one direction).

• Most people have no allergic reaction to base metals that are plated (standard for costume jewelry); however, if you're designing for someone who may be sensitive, you may want to use 14K gold, gold-filled, or sterling silver findings to eliminate the problem.

Where Do Good Ideas Come From?

That's the million dollar question! Every designer, no matter how talented, hits a dry spell once in a while. There are many places to get inspiration.

• **Television** — I like to watch mini-series just for the jewelry. Sometimes the show really stinks, but I can't tear myself away because the leading lady has 104 costume changes, each one with a different necklace! Period pieces have interesting jewelry.

I also love to watch those shopping-at-home channels. They have lovely, elegant jewelry. Many of the hosts are quite knowledgeable, and are very free to share useful information. I consider this a form of educational TV.

• **Women's Magazines** — Many of the high-fashion magazines are wonderful sources for design — models are selling $1,000 blouses, but look past that and see the terrific necklace she's wearing.

Even the "Working Mom" type of magazines will have great jewelry in them sometimes (I like the make-over sections where the after-pictures show fabulous jewelry to go with the new look).

• **Fine Department Stores** — I used to take my class on fieldtrips to the most exclusive department store in town, just to see the new jewelry. My students were very discreet, but it wasn't hard to tell that they were counting strands and making mental notes.

Everyone interprets their jewelry differently. In my classes, you can give 25 people the same bag of beads, yet end up with 25 different necklaces. No two are ever identical.

Design is so subjective. You could show the same hank of seedbeads to two people, and one will say, "Size 11°? TOO small!" yet the other will say "Oh, those Size 11°'s are HUGE!" Some like to design with beads 4mm or smaller; some will only work with 10mm on up!

So, what do you do if you hit a dry-spell? Have "Beader's Block"? The best thing you can do is have a cup of tea, put your beads in front of you, and the inspiration will come. If you ask a sculptor, he will say the finished statue exists in the block of marble, he just removes all of the extra. It's kind of like that with the beads — the finished necklace is sitting in your beadbox, you just need to rearrange it without the extra stuff to see it!

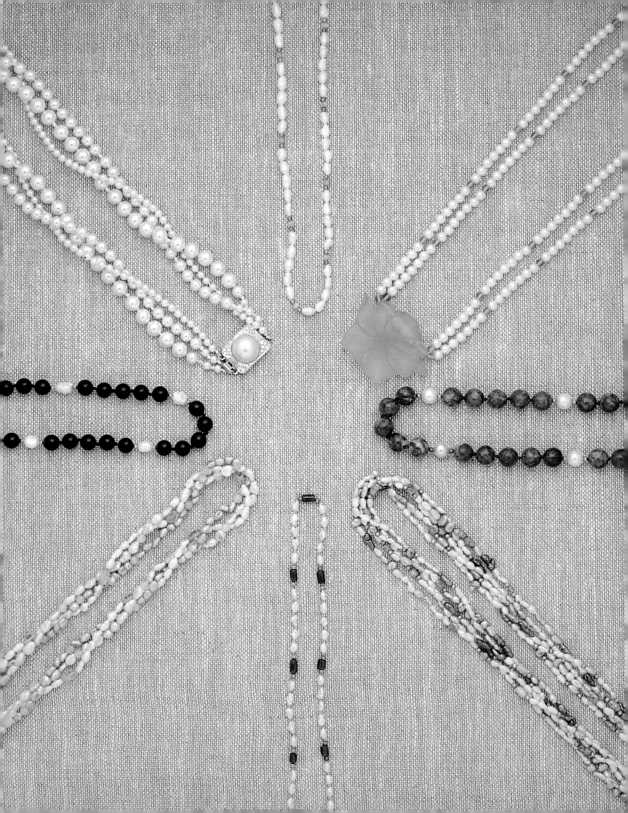

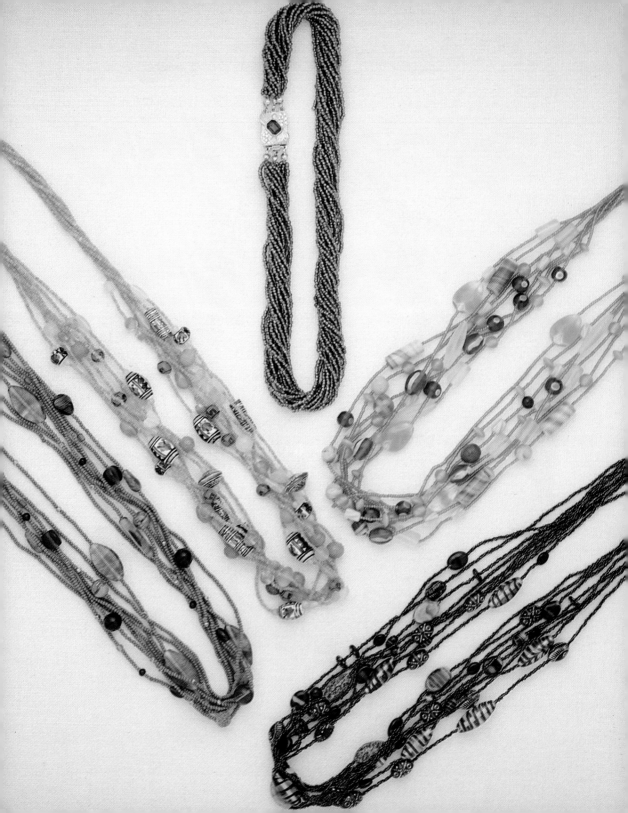

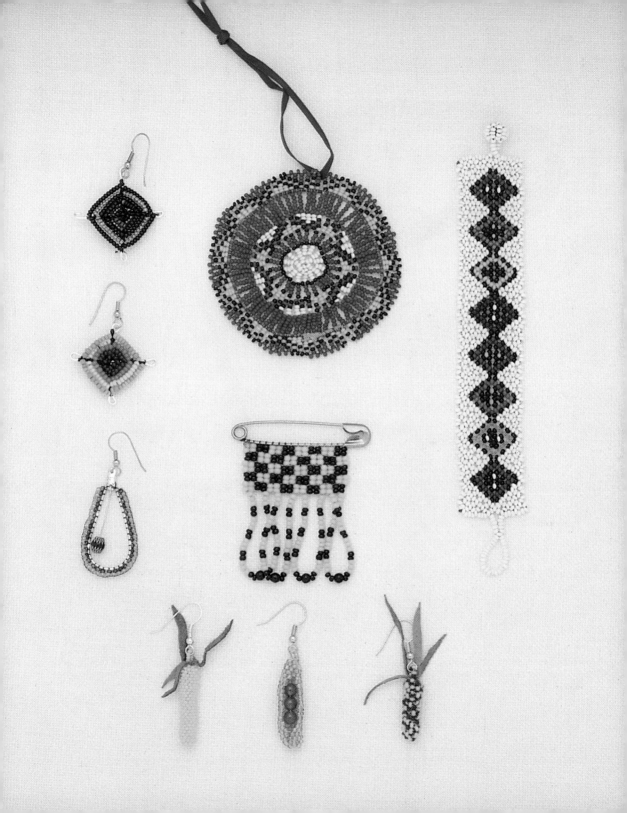

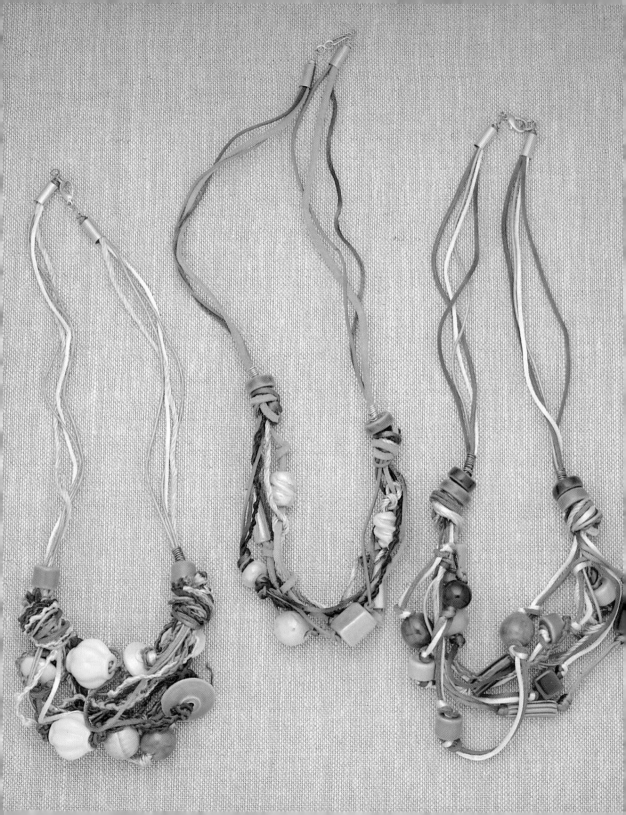

Color Photo Index

Page 49: Wire Necklaces
Page 50: Memory Wire Necklace & Bracelets
Page 51: Citrine & Garnet Necklace
Amethyst & Pearl Collar
Multi-Strand Rose Quartz
Continuous Strand
Page 52: Pearl Multi Strand Necklaces
Page 53: Single Strand Necklaces
Continuous Strand Necklaces
Multi-Strand Necklaces
Page 54: Southwest Necklace
Faux Zuni Necklace
Turquoise Necklace
Page 55: Variations of Southwest Necklace
Page 56: Single Strand Necklaces
Multi Strand Necklace
Native American Collar
Page 57: Woven Pink Crystal Necklace & Earring Set
Page 58: Woven Crystal Projects
Page 59: Needlewoven Projects
Page 60: Multi Strand Seedbead Necklaces
Page 61: Various Seedbead Projects
Page 62: Fringed Seedbead Necklace
Page 63: Various Seedbead Projects
Page 64: Medicine Pouch
Beaded Brooch
Circular Peyote Stitch
Page 65: Various Earrings
Page 66: Watchbands
Page 67: Hat Pins
Page 68: Polymer Clay
Page 69: Fantasy Necklace
Page 70: Zucchini Necklaces
Page 71: Glass Molded in Microwave
Page 72: Semi Precious Stones

FRONT COVER: Loomed Necklace
BACK COVER: Pi Woven Necklace and Peyote Stitch Spoon

Simple Earrings

Simple earrings are probably the quickest, easiest, least expensive jewelry you can make. The supplies cost next to nothing . . . and you only need 2 of everything. If you make them yourself, it's quite easy to have a pair for every outfit you own.

If you make them for selling, they can be a very profitable item. Either way, they're fast and fun, and you can make a pair in a little over a minute, once you get the hang of it.

You Need:

- Round nosed pliers
- Wire cutters
- 2 ear wires of any kind (pierced or unpierced)
- 2 pins, either head or eye
- 2 each of any beads you choose

Remember: whatever metaltone you choose to work with (goldtone, silvertone, etc.), it's best if you keep it consistent within the piece.

Step One:

Thread beads on pin in desired order (do this twice and make both earrings equal)

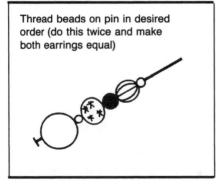

Step Two:

Cut pins with wire cutters 1/2 inch from top of bead.

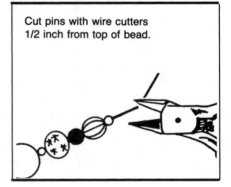

Step Three:

Bend the top of post to 90°
angle with round nose pliers

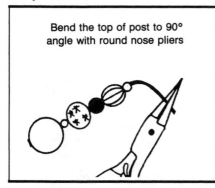

Step Four:

Thread the ear wire on the post

Step Five:

With round nose pliers, bend
the post in the *opposite direction*
to form a loop. (this gives a more
rounded and even loop)

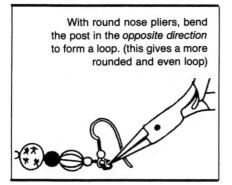

Step Six:

Close the loop

That's it!

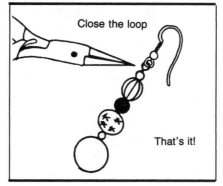

Variations of Simple Earrings

Now that you've mastered the basic wire bend, the possibilities are endless. Using the previous technique, you can incorporate different findings to expand your design potential.

• Incorporate findings that turn your single strand earring into a multistrand.

• There are findings made especially for this, or you can use bracelet or necklace end bars for the same purpose.

• Link together several short lengths of eye pins for movement.

• Connect your eye pins in different geometric shapes.

• Use metal charms/ornaments with your beads for different looks

• Thread your beads on circle crimps, continuous hoop earrings, or loops you've made yourself with wire, and attach to earwires.

• Utilize chain in your designs. You can lengthen the earring by using several chain/bead combinations, or you can create a "grape-cluster" effect by attaching several head pins with beads on them through the links of a chain (please see the section on chain as to which ones work best).

Looped Wire Earrings

CHINESE COIN EARRING

Wirebending designs really enhance your earrings. This one uses a Chinese coin with semiprecious beads, and has a museum-quality look.

Supplies Needed:
- Two Chinese coins
- 24 gauge wire
- Six small "Pi" (annular) beads
- Two earwires
- One chain nose plier

Step One:

Cut a 6" length of wire and fold in half. Insert bent end into hole in coin.

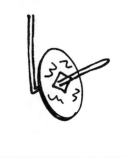

Step Two:

Catch wire ends in loop like a "half-hitch" knot.

Step Three:

Thread on 3 of your Pi beads. Using your pliers, loop wire into coil, catching your earwire. Cut off excess wire.

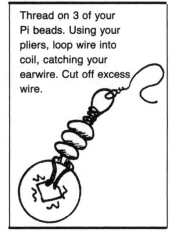

SOUTHWEST TURQUOISE PI EARRING

This earring employs exactly the same technique as the previous earring, but uses a silver feather and a turquoise Pi bead to give a very different look.

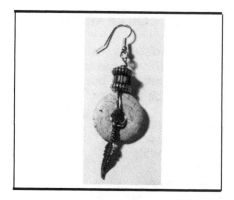

Supplies Needed:
- Two turquoise Pi beads
- 24 gauge wire
- Two small silver feathers
- Two earwires
- Two narrow trade beads
- Four metal rondells
- One chain nose plier

The only difference in this and the above earring is the substitution of beads used. As you can see, the effects are very different. Try other combinations of beads for other exciting looks.

ANOTHER VARIATION:

To make a very interesting earring, try threading your beads on a very long eye pin with your first bead that you thread on to be the top (upside down from the Simple Earring). Thread on a large Pi bead, bend the wire up, and coil it around the shaft of the eye pin. Attach your earwire to the top existing loop of the eye pin.

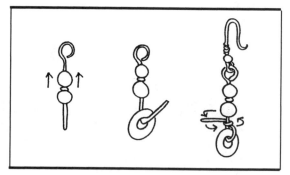

There are hundreds of other variations!

Wire Chain Necklace

This necklace uses very few beads . . . it's a great way to use up odds and ends! You're basically making your own chain as you work. The impact is in the way that the wire is bent and coiled, and the beads really stand out.

Supplies Needed:
- Two chain nose pliers
- Twenty to thirty beads
- 24 gauge wire
- One clasp

Step One:

Work right from the spool of wire. Thread a bead onto the wire, and make a loop in the wire (bend it back, with about 3" lead end).

Step Two:

Hold your wire with one plier, and grab the wire end with the other.

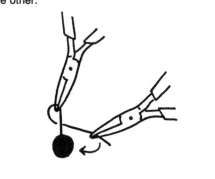

Step Three:

Twist the end around the wire shaft in a smooth, tight motion.

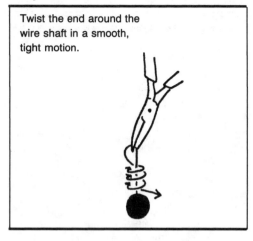

Step Four:

Trim off the excess wire from your looped end.

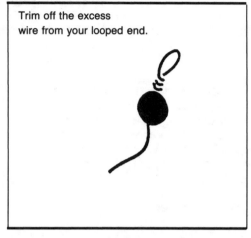

Step Five:

Keeping the bead with your finished loop, cut the wire from the spool 3'' from the bead (It helps to have that 3'' for gripping and control).
Your loops will look better if you work with excess wire that you can trim away.

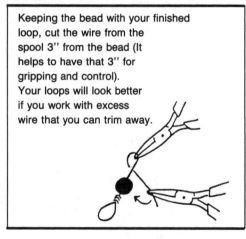

Step Six:

You now have a modular component. You'll repeat this sequence, and don't forget to catch the previous finished bead/wire component in your loop as you work.

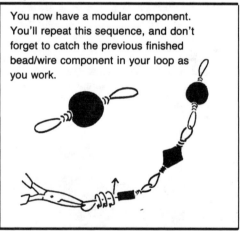

Rosaries

Making a Rosary is very easy, and makes a very special gift. Originally, the beads of the Rosary represented the prayers that priests must memorize.

When you make your own Rosary, you can choose your beads to have special significance: birthstones of family members, your grandmother's antique crystal, beads bought on a special day, or your favorite color. You can make them into a standard Rosary, or design a Rosary necklace to wear for special occasions.

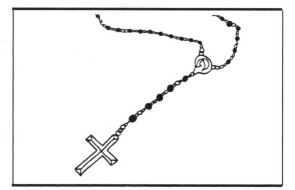

Supplies Needed:
- Fifty beads of one type (main bead)
- Nine beads that are similar or different (spacer bead)
- 20 gauge wire
- One crucifix
- One Rosary centerpiece
- One chain nose plier
- Sixteen jump rings

Step One:

You can link your Rosary with simple loops. Your pattern is 10 main beads, one jump ring, one spacer bead, one jump ring, 10 main beads, one jump ring, one spacer bead, one jump ring, 10 main beads, one jump ring, one spacer bead, one jump ring, 10 main beads, one jump ring, one spacer bead, one jump ring, 10 main beads. Be sure that it begins and ends with the 10 main beads.

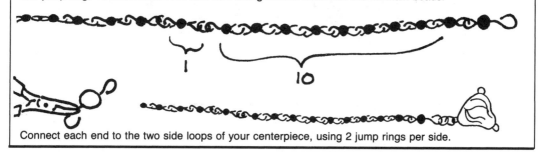

Connect each end to the two side loops of your centerpiece, using 2 jump rings per side.

Step Three:

Make a small separate length of beads by joining your five remaining spacer beads. The three center ones will link together, but you will use a jump ring to join the outer ones on each side. You'll then use your remaining jump rings to join this length to the bottom loop of the centerpiece, and the other end to the crucifix.

Charm Necklaces

A nice way to utilize chain in your designs is to attach charms and pretty beads to a nice chain, using head or eye pins. You can mix many variations: an "Eqyptian" theme where you've mixed charms of ankhs, pyramids, cartouches, scarabs, etc. with beads; a "Peruvian" theme where you've mixed the brightly colored Peruvian beads with the traditional charms; even mixing antique beads with old gum machine toys!

Your charms are joined with jump rings; your eye or head pins are made the same way you made your Simple Earrings, but threaded through the loops of the chains (please see the section on CHAINS to know which ones will work).

Supplies Needed:
- Miscellaneous charms
- Assortment of beads
- Jump rings
- Eye or head pins

How to Do It:

Thread your beads on your eye or head pins. Make several designs, just as you would make earrings. Thread them through the links of the chain, alternating with the charms. Make it as full as you like. Try using different lengths of chain for different effects.

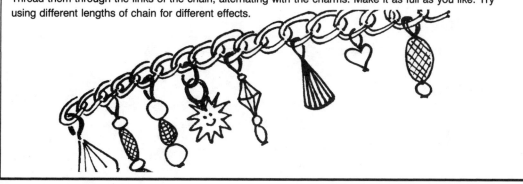

Using Jump Rings

Jump rings are a MUST for your bead box! They are the solution to many design problems. They are used for adding clasps and charms; for joining two findings that don't open to accommodate each other; for linking chain . . . the list goes on and on.

When working with jump rings, you want to keep their limitations in mind:

• Everytime you add a jump ring, you make a perpendicular connection. There may be times when you need to add two jump rings to keep the flow of design smooth (this is the situation many times with earrings).

• You must NEVER open a jump ring by pulling it open: it ruins the integrity of the curve, and you will never get it back to normal. Instead, swivel it sideways to open, then swivel it back to close.

• There are times when a jump ring might pull out from the weight of what you're connecting. You may need to upgrade to a split ring (just like what you use on your key ring, but smaller). This is made much stronger.

THE CONNECTED SEGMENT NECKLACE

Supplies Needed:
- Fifteen filigree segments, appx. 1'' square
- Thirty-two jump rings
- One clasp
- Chain nose plier

How to Do It:

Using your jump rings, connect each segment in two places. Finish by adding a clasp.

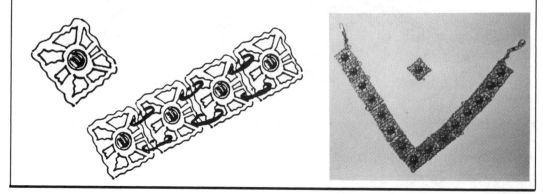

Bent Wire Rings

Rings are actually very easy to bead. One of my favorite projects involves wirebending rings. The first time I made these, my family was shocked at how easy they were to make, yet how elegant they looked!

Supplies Needed:
- 18 gauge wire
- 24 gauge wire
- Assortment of beads
- Two chain nose pliers
- Wire cutters
- A wooden dowel, about ¾ inches in diameter

Step One:

Cut a 2'' piece of 18 gauge wire and wrap it loosely around your dowel. This makes a nice curve for your ring. Now, readjust for sizing.

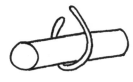

Step Two:

Using your pliers, bend the wire to form a small loop at one end. Cut the wire to fit ¾ of the way around your finger, then bend the second end in a small loop.

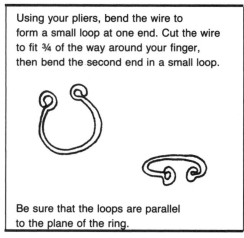

Be sure that the loops are parallel to the plane of the ring.

Step Three:

Thread beads on a length of 24 gauge wire. Wrap the end smoothly thru the loop of the 18 gauge, and coil carefully.

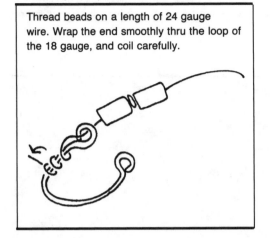

Step Four:

Thread the other end of the wire thru the other loop of the 18 gauge, and coil tightly to match the other side.

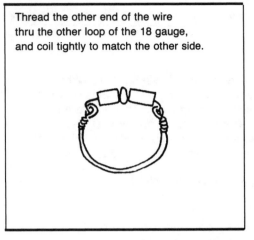

Experiment with different beads and different ratios of 18 gauge to 24 gauge wire. Sometimes you'll want lots of beads, sometimes just a few.

Here's a guide to ring sizes that should help your designs. Trace this so you can cut it out and see your size.

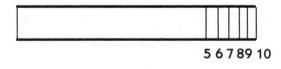

5 6 7 89 10

RING SIZES

Woven Wire Rings

This is one of the first bead projects I ever remember doing. It's so easy and fun, a child can do it!

Supplies Needed:
- 28 gauge wire
- Assortment of seedbeads
- Wire cutters

Step One:

Cut a one foot length of wire. Thread on 3 seedbeads.

Step Two:

Center the beads on the wire. Bend up the sides, and add 3 more seedbeads. Crisscross your wire through the seedbeads.

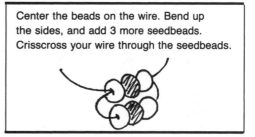

Step Three:

Keep working like so, adding beads and criss-crossing wire through them. If you want a ring that widens at the top, experiment with different effects by adding beads, two at a time. When you have the right length, then you are done. Weave the ends together, being sure not to leave any exposed wire, and trim.

Memory Wire Collar & Bracelet

Memory Wire is a marvelous wire that holds its coiled shape. It can be used for bracelets and necklaces (the diameters are different for each). It's quick and easy to use, and doesn't need a clasp. The bracelet is worked in one continuous length of wire; the necklace is cut into three strands and joined together by separator bars. It is recommended that you do not use long lengths of necklace wire because of the possibility of getting it wound on too tightly.

Supplies Needed:

- 20" bracelet coil memory wire
- 48" necklace coil memory wire
- 11 separator bars (with rhinestones preferred)
- 67 rhinestone rondells
- 61 7mm round crystal beads
- Two 16" strands of 7mm pearls
- Round nose plier
- Wire cutter
- Head pins (optional)

THE BRACELET

Step One:

Using your round nose plier, make a loop in one end of the wire. Thread your beads on in the order of your pattern.

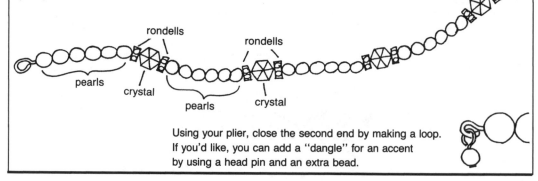

rondells

rondells

pearls

crystal

pearls

crystal

Using your plier, close the second end by making a loop. If you'd like, you can add a "dangle" for an accent by using a head pin and an extra bead.

THE COLLAR:

Strand Number One:

Cut the necklace coil into three equal lengths, using your wire cutter. Make a loop at the end, and thread beads on in your pattern.

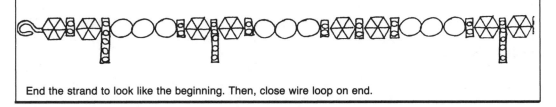

End the strand to look like the beginning. Then, close wire loop on end.

Strand Number Two:

Match the pattern of the first strand. When you get to the separator bars, thread the wire through the second hole. Also, you'll need to add other separator bars to connect to the third strand. Don't forget to position them all in the same direction (facing the same way)! When the strand is done, close the second end in a loop.

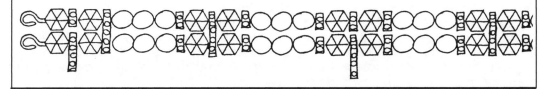

Strand Number Three:

Complete the pattern to match with the third strand. If you'd like, you can add a dangle to the bottom strand.

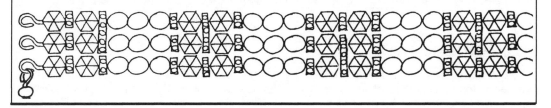

VARIATIONS:

• Try using a variety of beads on both collar and bracelet for different effects (see page 50 for ideas).

Wire Bending

There are many styles of wire bending, and many types of wire that can be used. The effects can be both subtle and dramatic, and anyone who can grip a plier can do fantastic wirework.

TYPES OF WIRE

Wire is available in 14K gold (which is very soft), gold-filled, gold-plated, sterling, sterling-plated, and jeweler's wire (which comes in gold, silver, copper, red, and green, but is not a precious metal). You can also use the junky stuff from the hardware store, or even old telephone cable (I love the striped ones).

Wire can be round, flat, square, or oval.

The gauges of wire are very confusing! The higher the number gauge, the thinner the wire (in other words, 18 gauge is thicker than 20 gauge, which is thicker than 24 gauge, which is thicker than 28 gauge). There are other gauges available, too.

One of the most enjoyable times I ever had was working in my friend's workshop, making my own silver wire. It was a very involved process, where you have to flatten the wire into a thin pancake (sort of like a pasta press, but a lot harder to turn the wheel!); then you had to draw the wire to get it to the right gauge. I developed a healthy respect for people who do this quite often!

Jeweler's wire cannot be drawn, nor can plated wire. If you are not working with a precious metal wire, than it is best to purchase the correct gauge. Some wires have been treated to keep their shape better. They will be harder to work with, but will not warp as badly. The wires that are soft or semi-soft might adjust themselves to get out of shape. It is important to choose the right wire for the technique you are using.

POSAMENTERIE STYLE

Taken from the German word for lace-work, Posament, this beautiful, lacy pattern of wirebending does resemble lace. It dates back to the 9th century B.C. (Central European Late Bronze Age).

You can design pins, necklace parts, earrings, findings, etc. using this technique.

POSAMENTERIE BROOCH

Supplies Needed:
- Flattened wire band, appx. 1/8" wide and 1 foot long
- 22 gauge wire
- One cabochon
- Hot glue gun
- One brooch back
- One of each plier: chain nose, round nose, and duckbill

Step One:

One by one, you'll coil the 22 gauge wire into decorative swirls. Plan a design before beginning, to minimize wear-and-tear on the wire.

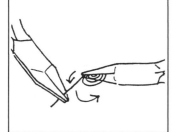

Step Two:

If you want a "flattened" look, and you're using a precious metal wire, you can flatten the coils by placing your wirework under a wooden block and *carefully* hammering.

Step Three:

Gather your design together, and carefully wrap your flattened band tightly around it to hold it in place.

Step Four:

Take 2 pieces of 22 gauge wire, and twist them together. Make a frame around your cabochon.

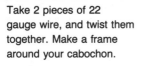

Step Five:

Using your glue gun, assemble the brooch with the cabochon on top.

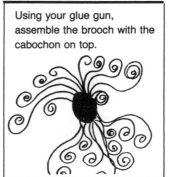

Step Six:

Hot glue the pinback to the brooch.

Wrap your wire around household items to achieve special effects. Pencils, other gauges of wire, and square tubing are just some of what can be used.

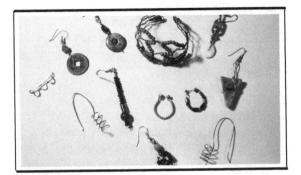

The variety of techniques is amazing!

Technique One:

Wirebend a pierced earring hoop that needs no additional findings.

Technique Two:

Make your own custom earwires with swirls and coils

Technique Three:

Make your own kilt pins

Technique Four:

Make your own hook-and-eye clasps for leather or rattail necklaces.

Technique Five:

Freeform wirebend a cage for a stone

Technique Six:

Wrap wire around other wire to make tiny little coils

THE BEST LITTLE BEADING BOOK

Basic Stringing Techniques — Single Strand

There are many ways to string your necklaces, bracelets, anklets, etc, and it's very confusing to know which is the best to use for your particular project. At one time or other, we've all had that sinking feeling as our beautiful creation comes apart and bounces away, in pieces. The solution is to take a minute or two to analyze the piece before you begin, so you'll know which is the best way to put it together.

There are many factors to take into account. Are the beads heavy? Are they faceted or sharp? How large are the holes in the beads? How do you want this to hang — to drape softly, or hang rigidly? Where is this to be worn?

There are several things you should NEVER string with. Dental floss is biodegradable; fishing line is heat reactive (heat dries it out and it breaks); cotton stretches, and over time, will rot.

The most popular stringing media includes "**TIGER TAIL**", **SILK THREAD,** and **NYLON THREAD.**

The easiest medium for a beginner (and the preferred medium of many professionals) is "tiger tail". That's a nickname given to a wire that's been encased in a nylon cable. It has several thicknesses, so you can use the thinnest for smaller beads (.012), medium weights for medium beads (.015, .018), and the heaviest weights for heavy beads (.020, .024).

Tiger tail is recommended for very heavy beads that would stretch or cut a thread (like leaded crystal, or large heavy semi-precious stones). It's also great for ankle bracelets and necklaces for people who wear their necklaces when they swim.

Being a wire, tiger tail cannot be knotted (it will kink and break). It's used with "crimp beads". These are small beads designed to be crushed into position at the ends of the piece. They have little teeth inside, and once crushed (or "crimped"), these teeth imbed into the nylon coating of the tiger tail and form a non-slip ending. There's also crimp tubes, which work the same way, but are long and smooth.

You don't need a needle when you work with tiger tail. For each strand you make, you'll need tiger tail, 4 crimp beads, your beads, and a chain nose plier or crimping plier (a special plier made just for crimping — it's well worth buying, because it really does make it easier). It also helps to have scotch tape on hand.

The way to work with tiger tail is:

Step One:

Cut a length of tiger tail 12'' longer than your intended necklace. Adhere scotch tape to one end.

Step Two:

String your beads onto the tigertail. If you change your mind or make a mistake, simply remove the tape if necessary and remedy, without having to remove every bead you just strung.

Step Three:

Add 2 crimp beads on the end, your clasp, and return the tigertail back thru the crimp beads. Make sure that you leave enought tigertail to complete the second side.

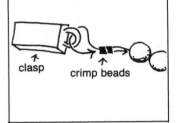

clasp   crimp beads

Step Four:

With a plier, crush the crimp beads. Be careful that they're where you want them to be, and that your clasp hasn't wandered into the grip of the pliers (it'll crush)

If possible, feed the tiger tail back thru some of the beads.

Step Five:

Let the strand hang vertically (clasp open) to help remove kinks from the tiger tail. Carefully run your hand. down the strand to smooth out any remaining kinks.

Step Six:

Repeat like the first side. (2 crimps, the clasp, and back through the crimps, adjusting the tension. Now, crimp carefully.

trim

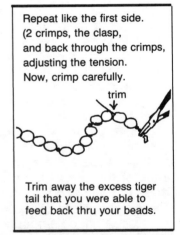

Trim away the excess tiger tail that you were able to feed back thru your beads.

Don't use tiger tail for pearls, or very small beads (being a wire, it will have a life of its own). Be careful not to kink it as you work with it, because the kink will always be there.

When you storing jewelry that you've strung on tigertail, it's best to lay it flat, coiled with the clasp open. If you wad it up, it will kink and never hang right. If you store it by hanging it, gravity will do to it what it does to all of us: it will start to sag. Always store your jewelry laying flat.

THE BEST LITTLE BEADING BOOK

These crystal necklaces were made with tiger tail, because of the sharpness of the crystal beads.

These very large amethyst posed a real challenge! They're so heavy, they kept breaking even the heaviest of tiger tail. The solution was to string them with two strands of tiger tail, and to use extra large crimps (like a regular crimp, but larger, to hold two strands). The ends were then hidden under end cones to give a more polished look.

Stringing with a Thread

For pearls and most semi precious beads, silk or nylon bead cord are recommended. You want to calibrate the thread to the size of the hole in the bead. Your goal is to fill the holes up with the largest possible thread to eliminate friction, which will result in your piece rubbing on the thread and breaking. You always want to work with your thread doubled, as this will strengthen the piece.

For silk or nylon thread, you'll need a needle (either the twisted wire kind with the collapsible eye, or a plastic dental flossing needle — if this fits through your beads, it's really easy to thread). You'll also need knot covers, also known as bead tips.

There are three types of knot covers. Two of them are useful, the third is not. The two best ones are a clamshell style, and a knotcup. You may sometimes hear knot covers referred to as "bead tips".

With the knotcup, your knot is visible. You have to make a very perfect knot, because it shows. It is considered traditional to use the knotcup with pearls.

With the clamshell style, the knot is hidden. There's a little hole in the hinge, and after you anchor and cement your knot, you close the clamshell. I recommend this style, because your knot could look like heck, but when you close the clamshell, no one knows.

The third style is called a cullotte. It looks almost just like the clamshell, except that the hole is not in the hinge, but on the side. The problem with this is that there is really nothing to anchor that knot inside, and the weight of the necklace can pull out the knot (and the necklace falls apart!) in no time at all.

There's also French bullion for your ends, which takes a little practice to work with it and get the results you like. We'll get to that in a minute.

To string on silk thread or bead cord:

First of all, figure the length of thread needed. To do this, take the length of the finished piece, add 12", then double. (For example: to make a 24" necklace, take 24" of silk, add 12" (36") and double. You'll need 72". You'll work double thread, and you'll need extra to manipulate your endings, which accounts for the extra inches figured.

The following method is for stringing WITHOUT knotting between each bead. Please see the following section for BEAD KNOTTING.

Step One:

Thread your needle, and make an overhand knot using both tails of the thread.

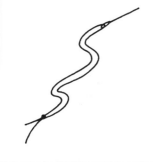

Step Two:

Add the first knot cover, with the needle going from inside to outside. If done properly, the cup part of the knot cover is covering the knot. The loop is facing out.

Step Three:

Add your beads, then the second knot cover, in the opposite direction than the first.

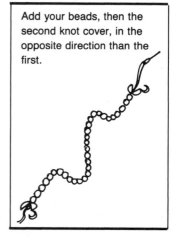

Step Four:

Make a couple of square knots tightly in the clamshell of the knot cover.

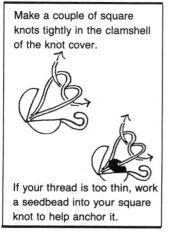

If your thread is too thin, work a seedbead into your square knot to help anchor it.

Step Five:

Cement the knots inside the knot cover, and carefully close. (If you've used a seedbead, make sure it's lying flat, so your knot cover will close completely)

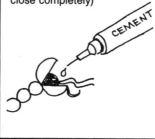

Step Six:

Let the cement dry, then snip off the extra thread.

Use the little hook on the knotcover to attach your clasp.

Daisy Necklace

Part of what makes this necklace so unusual is the toggle clasp with hanging charm in the front.

Supplies Needed:
- One strand each of peridot, garnets, and amber chips
- Two flower findings
- One large daisy finding (or other charm)
- One large toggle clasp
- Two clamshell-style knot covers
- 46 2mm sterling silver beads
- One twisted wire needle
- 2½ yards of silk thread, size "F"
- One chain nose plier
- Four ¼" jumprings, and one 3/8" jumpring
- Cement

Step One:

You'll work with your thread doubled. Thread your needle, and add your knot cover. Remember: when you use a knot cover, you want the clamshell to cover the knot. It's very easy to put in on in the wrong direction.

Step Two:

When working with chips, you measure by the inch, not the number of chips. The pattern is as follows:
3 garnets, 1 silver bead, ½" of amber, 1 silver bead, ½" of peridot, 1 silver bead, 1 garnet, 1 silver bead, ½" of peridot, etc. Keep repeating, ending with the same pattern as at the beginning.

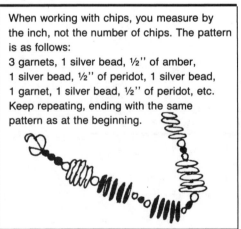

Step Three:

End with the knot cover. Remember: your ends should look like mirror images (opposite to each other).

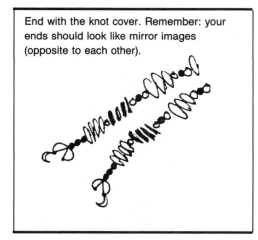

Step Four:

Cement the knot in the knot cover, and use your pliers to close. Cut off your excess thread.

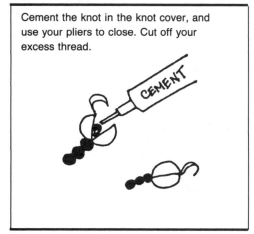

Step Five:

Attach the loop on each knot cover to each of the flower findings.

Step Six:

Attach the flower findings to the toggle clasp, using one small jumpring on the ring side, and three small jumprings on the bar side.

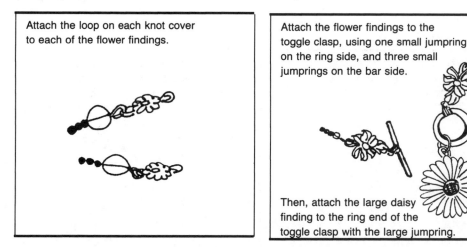

Then, attach the large daisy finding to the ring end of the toggle clasp with the large jumpring.

A very simple and elegant necklace! Try using other charms and findings in place of the daisy for a very different look.

Leaf Necklace

This elegant necklace is very easy to make. The leaves that hang down are actually strung on head pins.

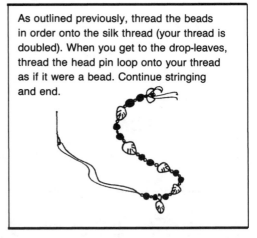

Supplies Needed:

- Thirteen semiprecious leaf-shaped beads
- Twenty-two 8mm black onyx beads
- Thirty-two 2½mm gold spacer beads
- Two knot covers
- One clasp
- Three head pins
- 1½ yards "F" weight silk
- 1 twisted wire needle
- Cement

Step One:

As if you were making an earring, thread the leaf on a head pin and close the loop.

Step Two:

As outlined previously, thread the beads in order onto the silk thread (your thread is doubled). When you get to the drop-leaves, thread the head pin loop onto your thread as if it were a bead. Continue stringing and end.

VARIATIONS:

The following necklaces were all strung in the same manner; the only difference is the beads that are used.

CRYSTAL AND CARNELIAN NECKLACE

Materials Needed:

- One strand of side-drilled crystal
- One strand of 4mm carnelian
- 1½ yards "F" weight silk
- One clasp
- Two knot covers
- Cement

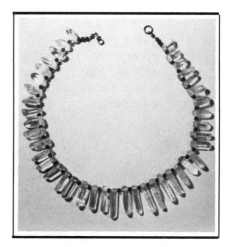

ROSE QUARTZ MAXI-COLLAR NECKLACE

Materials Needed:

- One maxi-collar set
- One strand of 4mm rose quartz
- 1½ yards "F" weight silk
- One clasp
- Two knot covers
- Cement

THE BEST LITTLE BEADING BOOK

SNOWFLAKE OBSIDIAN MOON & STAR CHOKER

Materials Needed:

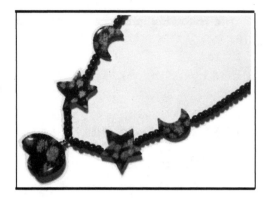

- Two each of snowflake obsidian moons and stars
- One obsidian fetish bear
- One strand of size 6° seedbeads ("E" beads)
- One head pin
- 1½ yards "F" weight silk
- One clasp
- Two knot covers
- Cement

CRYSTAL WITH ANTIQUE FINDINGS

Experiment with attaching your knot covers to antique findings of different types. Old bits of broken necklaces, shoe buckles, old belt buckles, etc.

ANOTHER VARIATION:

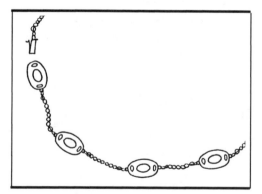

You can make extenders for necklaces by incorporating several clasps into one necklace. The same necklace can then be worn as a long or short necklace, depending on the number of segments you include.

THE BEST LITTLE BEADING BOOK

Adjustable Length Necklace

The nice thing about this kind of necklace is that it will fit everybody without sacrificing the style!

Supplies Needed:

- Forty 3½mm silver beads
- Ten 4mm black onyx beads
- Thirty 4x6mm malachite tube-shaped beads
- One main piece
- A four-inch length of chain
- One size 11° black seedbead
- One lobster clasp
- Two knot covers
- 1½ yards "F" weight silk
- 1 twisted wire needle
- Cement

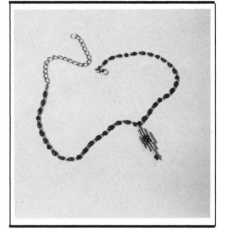

Step One:

Double your thread and start threading your beads as usual.

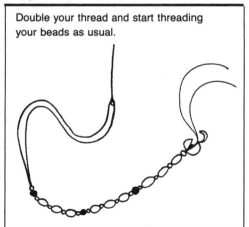

Step Two:

When you get to the half-way point, thread on your main piece, then your seedbead, then back up through the mainpiece. It doesn't hurt to make a knot on either side of the mainpiece to help stabilize it.

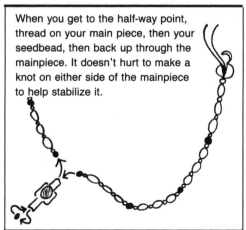

Step Three:

Finish with your knot covers (cement and close) when done stringing, and attach to the chain.

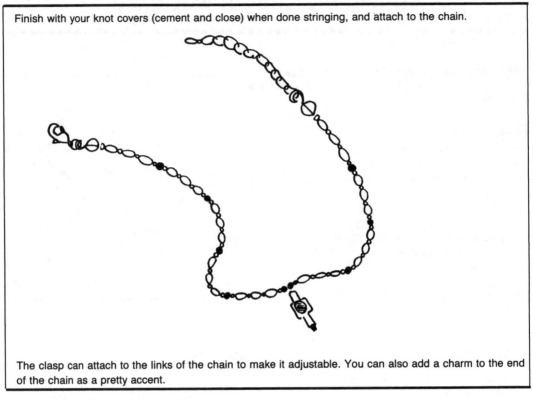

The clasp can attach to the links of the chain to make it adjustable. You can also add a charm to the end of the chain as a pretty accent.

Eye Glass Holders

These can actually be strung on either tiger tail or thread. If it will suffer lots of abuse, you may choose to use the tiger tail; although the thread has more of a flow to it.

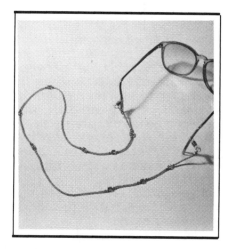

Supplies Needed:

- Turquoise seedbeads
- Nine tube-shaped amethyst beads
- Eighteen brushed gold accent beads
- Two knot covers
- Eye glass connectors
- Two yards "F" weight silk
- One twisted wire needle
- Cement

How To Do It:

String this exactly as you would a necklace (with your thread doubled), then attach your knot covers to the eyeglass connectors.

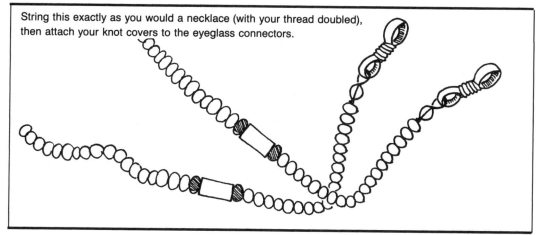

Knotting Between Beads

The mark of a fine necklace is sometimes judged by whether or not the beads have been knotted between. Fine pearls are always knotted; many semi-precious and glass beads are also. How do you know when to knot between the beads?

If the beads are to be strung on silk or nylon thread, and you want a more elegant look, then you can knot between them. You should not knot between beads that are smaller than 4mm, or very small fresh water pearls, or between seedbeads (we call this obsessive-compulsive. Unless this is satisfying a need of some kind, don't knot between beads that small).

If your beads are funky and rough, it's a contradiction in design to knot between them as you would pearls.

One of the main functions of knotting is to keep beads from rubbing together. So, if you're using delicate beads (like pearls) it may be a good idea to knot.

If you just inherited Aunt Minnie's pearl necklace, but half the beads are gone, then knotting can be a way to extend the beads you have and make the necklace longer.

How do you know how much thread is needed when you're knotting?

Your knots will take up approximately 1/8" each. In other words, every eight knots will add one inch. (This can differ, depending on knotting style and thickness of thread). When you knot, you always have one more knot than the number of beads.

Now, let's say you went to the gem show and they had a very special strand of something that you've never seen before. It was very expensive, so you didn't want to buy more than you need, but you're not sure if this is enough to make a necklace that would be long enough. How do you know?

Well, if you have a 16" strand of beads, and the beads run 4 to the inch, you then have 64 beads, and 65 knots.

Your beads = 16"

Your knots = 8"

Your clasp/knot covers = 1"
_____

Your necklace = 25"

You can plug in any numbers for this formula to work. With this method, you'll know if you need extra beads before you start.

You can also say:

I have 21 beads that are 5mm, which is appx. 5 beads to the inch. How long will this end up?

$$21 \text{ beads} = \text{appx. } 4''$$
$$22 \text{ knots} = \text{appx. } 3''$$
$$\text{Your clasp/knot covers} = \text{appx. } 1''$$
$$\overline{}$$
$$\text{This strand would only equal } 8''$$

If it's not going to be a bracelet, then you better think about mixing in some other beads!

Now that you know the length the beads will end up, now you should start thinking about how much thread to work with. There's nothing worse than spending 3 days knotting a LONG strand of pearls, only to find that you're two inches short of thread at the end! There are several ways to knot, and that dictates how much thread you will need.

Some basic information that works for all of the methods is:

• NEVER wax any thread that's going into a necklace, unless you're weaving seedbeads and need the strength (not the case here!). If you wax the thread and then knot, three things will occur: (1) on a hot day, the wax will melt and run out onto the clothes of the wearer; (2) the wax will harden and discolor at some point, and look like heck; and (3) the next person who has to cut the threads apart and restring will hate you for waxing — once the wax hardens, you have to ream out EACH BEAD with a needle (yuk). Trust me — do not wax your thread when knotting!

• You should always try to work with your thread doubled — working single thread is just not strong enough, and can break in the future. Working double-thread gives you extra strength and a backup, should one thread break. Calibrate your thread thickness to the size of the hole of the bead. Always take your beads with you when buying thread, so you know you have the right weight. Remember: when you knot, the knot shouldn't slip into the beads; it should hold the bead in place; yet the thread also needs to be the right weight to go into the bead easily.

• If you find you're having difficulties with the thread going into the beads, yet you know that the thread is the right weight, instead try switching needles. Not all needles will be compatible with all beads. The twisted wire needles with collapsing eyes seem to work the best for most beads.

• It's best if your beads all have uniformly drilled holes in them — you will go crazy trying to find thread to work with both small and large holes.

• It's best not to try to make three knots in the same place when you find one knot isn't big enough. It's better to upgrade to a thicker thread.

• Always work as tightly as possible with your knots. Threads will stretch out, but they can never be shrunk properly.

• Always make your knots consistently in the same direction. If you knot this way and that, then the finished piece will hang funny.

METHOD ONE: THE TRADITIONAL ONE NEEDLE METHOD

You'll Need:

- Silk or nylon bead cord
- One twisted wire needle
- Beads of your choice
- Jeweler's fine point tweezers
- Scotch tape
- Knot covers
- Clasp
- Cement

Step One:

Thread your needle with the correct length of thread. Make an overhand knot in the ends. Add a knot cover. Tape this to the table in front of you (I tape on the right. You may find that taping to the left is easier).

Step Two:

Make an overhand knot just after your knot cover. This stabilizes the end. Use your tweezers. YOU MUST PUT THE TIP OF THE TWEEZER INTO THE LOOP OF THE OVERHAND KNOT FOR THIS TO WORK. The tweezer guides the knot down to the tip.

Step Three:

As you pull the end with the needle to tighten the knot, be aware of the way the thread should be traveling down the shaft of the tweezers, which should be lightly gripping the place where you want the knot to be. THE KNOT WILL END UP WHEREVER THE TIP OF THE TWEEZERS IS.

Step Four:

When you have pulled all the way, stop pulling the thread as you CAREFULLY pull out the tweezers. Then, take your two strands, and lift and separate them to pull the knot back against the knot cover, as closely as possible.

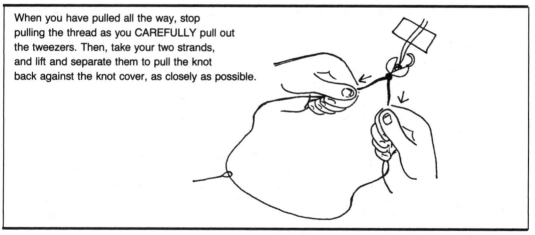

Step Five:

Add a bead, and repeat the same knotting process. Keep repeating until you have the desired length.

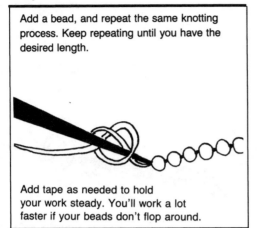

Add tape as needed to hold your work steady. You'll work a lot faster if your beads don't flop around.

Step Six:

When you get to the end, add your second knotcover, cement the knots and close. Attach your clasp.

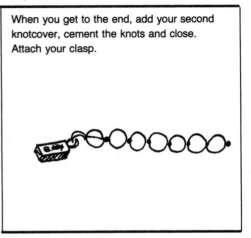

METHOD TWO: THE ONE NEEDLE METHOD, PRE-THREADED BEADS

You'll Need:

- Silk or nylon bead cord
- One twisted wire needle
- Beads of your choice
- Jeweler's fine point tweezers

- Scotch tape
- Knot covers
- Clasp
- Cement

Step One:

The biggest difference between this and the first method is that you pre-thread the beads unto your thread all at once before you begin to knot. The benefit is that you can't lose the beads when they're not loose. Start the same way, but pre-thread all beads.

Step Two:

After threading all the beads on the needle, make sure you have left at least one foot of thread between the knot cover and your pre-threaded strand. Starting with the needle, wrap this strand around a bobbin or piece of cardboard to keep it together.

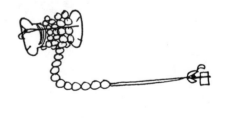

Step Three:

Dispense your beads one-at-a-time, as needed. This is actually quicker than the first method (add-a-bead, knot, add-a-bead, knot), but it's a little trickier, because your thread can tangle. The rest is the same. Practice will make perfect.

METHOD THREE: THE ONE NEEDLE METHOD, USING A PIN

You'll Need:

- Silk or nylon bead cord
- One twisted wire needle
- Beads of your choice
- Long hat pin or dress maker's pin
- Scotch tape
- Knot covers
- Clasp
- Cement

How-to-do-it:

The only difference here is that instead of using a tweezers, you can use a pin. You won't be gripping this like you do with the tweezers; you'll be pushing down in the loop to hold it in place. PRACTICE, PRACTICE, PRACTICE!

METHOD FOUR: THE TWO NEEDLE METHOD

You'll love this method . . . it doesn't use tweezers. However, your knots won't look as professional. For this procedure, you'll measure your thread a little differently. You'll cut two lengths of thread, each one is three times the finished length of the necklace.
For example: to make a 20" necklace, cut two lengths 60" long.

You'll Need:

- Silk or nylon bead cord
- Two twisted wire needles
- Beads of your choice
- Scotch tape
- Knot covers
- Clasp
- Cement

Step One:

Thread one needle on each length of thread.
Knot all four tails together.

Step Two:

One at a time, thread your needles through the first knot cover.

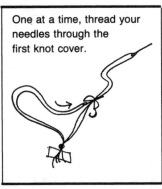

Step Three:

Make a square knot.

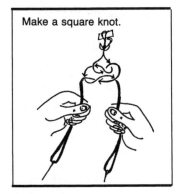

Step Four:

Now, alternately, add a bead by bringing both needles in the same direction through each bead, then making a square knot.

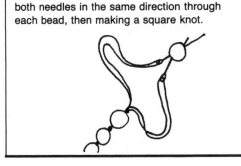

Step Five:

You'll end this strand like the others.

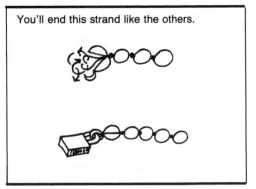

Working With Bullion

French Bullion (also known as French Coil) is an alternative method of ending your necklaces or bracelets. It's like a tiny little conduit for protecting your threads. It's very fragile by itself, and tends to stretch out of shape easily (when it's stretched, it looks like a long thin wire). It helps decrease the friction at the clasp which could prematurely break your necklace.

It's wonderful for ending very small fresh water pearls, fine pearls, or anytime you don't want a (relatively) large, overpowering knot cover taking away from small, delicate beads. French Bullion will not work well with heavy beads; it's meant to be used only with finer ones. It can be used for bracelets, watchbands, even earrings.

It comes in a couple of thicknesses, for both lighter-weight and medium-weight thread. You cannot use Bullion with tigertail.

HOW TO USE BULLION:

Step One:

Cut off ½ inch of Bullion. String one bead on your needle, then the Bullion.

Step Two:

Draw the Bullion and bead down to the tail end, away from the needle. Bend the Bullion in half, and make a square knot in the thread just outside of where the Bullion ends. Thread back through that first bead, and continue stringing.

Don't forget to add your clasp to the loop.

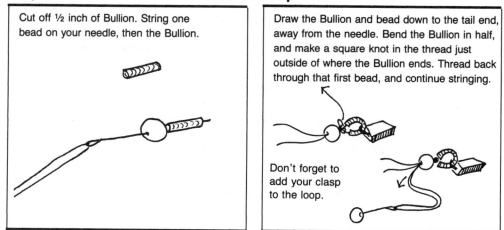

THE BEST LITTLE BEADING BOOK

Step Three:

If you've been knotting between your beads, when you get to three beads from the end, stop knotting, string on your Bullion, knot it, and go back through those last three beads, inserting overhand knots where there were no knots to make it look uniform. Cement and trim.

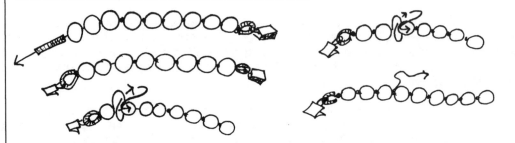

If you haven't been knotting between each bead, complete with the Bullion in the same way, but instead of adding knots, now you'll just backtrack through a few beads. Cement and trim.

●●

Working With A Magic Clasp

●●

This is by far the most frustrating clasp known to Mankind! It's comprised of two drilled-out beads; one end is the "male" end, and is threaded like a screw; the other is the "female" end, and has a hollowed out area that receives the threaded screw end. It's really tricky as to how to put it together!

Step One:

Measure your thread for stringing. Thread your needle, and, working with your thread doubled, make a knot in the ends right at the END of the thread. Cement completely now. When dry, trim off the excess thread beyond the knot (at the tail end). You should have a perfect little ball of a knot.

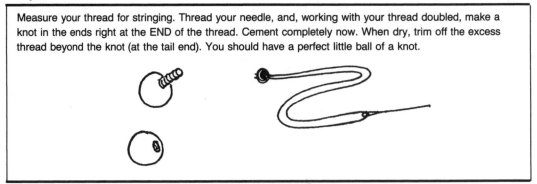

Step Two:

Remove the screw and thread ends from inside the Magic Clasp. Usually beads that have been prepped for this clasp have been specially drilled from two sides to the halfway point, so that one drilled side is bigger than the other. This is so that when you bring your knot through the clasp, it will catch where the difference occurs. It holds your knot in place; so you can then string your beads. Usually when a Magic Clasp is used, the beads are knotted between.

Measure your thread as usual, bring your needle thru the magic clasp, catching the knot. Continue stringing and knotting as you normally would.

Step Three:

When you are three beads from the end, string them on, but do not knot between them. Now is the tricky part! You need to cut a SMALL (1/16") piece of Bullion. Thread through the second end of the Magic Clasp, through the small piece of Bullion, and back out through the same hole in the clasp.

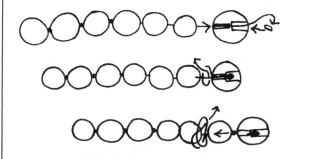

After you've completed the entire process, replace the threaded findings back into both Magic Clasp beads.

Make overhand knots around your strand to match your other knots. Cement and trim.

LIMITATIONS OF THE MAGIC CLASP:

• If you overdrill your beads, then they will no longer hold your thread inside.
• Plentiful use of cement is mandatory for this to hold.
• The way that the clasp assembly fits into the bead is kind of like a little "Molly-bolt". Take care that this does not loosen, as you shouldn't have to cement the clasp into the bead (this is limiting), it should hold in there by itself.

Combining Tiger Tail With Thread For Knotting

There will be times that you want the strength of tiger tail, but you want the look of the knots in between. What to do?

You can combine tiger tail with thread, but the trick is in knowing how. Remember: YOU CANNOT KNOT THE TIGER TAIL. ALL KNOTTING IS DONE IN THE THREAD. This method may seem strange, but it really does look nice when you're done.

You'll Need:

- Silk or nylon bead cord
- One twisted wire needle
- Beads of your choice
- Tiger tail in the weight of your choice
- Two crimp beads
- Scotch tape
- Clamshell style knot covers (only this type will work)
- Clasp
- Crimping plier
- Cement

Step One:

Thread your needle with the correct length of thread. Make an overhand knot in the ends. Add a knot cover. Take a length of tiger tail. Crimp on one crimp bead and feed this into the same knot cover.

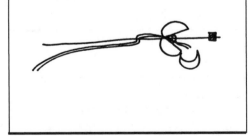

Step Two:

Make an overhand knot just after your knot cover, but hide the tigertail inside the knot.

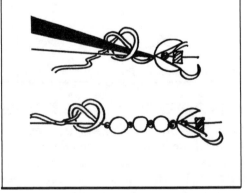

THE BEST LITTLE BEADING BOOK

Step Three:

Now, you can simultaneously thread through the beads with both tiger tail and thread, just make sure that you hide the tiger tail into the knots you are making.

When you're done, crimp a crimp bead into the second knot cover, and make your knot as usual with the thread. Cement the knotted thread, and close the knot covers. No one is the wiser as to what's inside!

They also call crimp beads "French Crimps" — that doesn't make them any prettier when they're crimped. You can also hide your crimp beads in a knot cover in this manner if you don't like the way the crimp beads look when squashed.

Making Continuous Necklaces Without Clasps

There are times that you may not want to put a clasp in a necklace. You can make continuous strands with both tiger tail and thread. Bear in mind: the necklace has to be long enough to go over your head without opening.

METHOD ONE: USING TIGER TAIL

You'll Need:

- Tiger tail
- Five crimp beads
- Beads of your choice
- Scotch tape
- Crimping pliers

Step One:

Place the tape on the end of the tiger tail, and thread all of the beads on as usual.

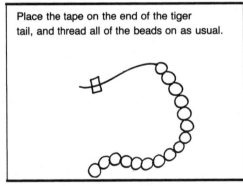

Step Two:

Near the ends, space out your five crimp beads every inch or so.

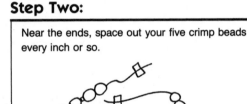

Step Three:

Bring your ends together, and crossover your tigertail in the beads and crimp beads for about 5 - 6'' (beyond all of your crimp beads.) Crush the crimp beads and trim the extra tiger tail away.

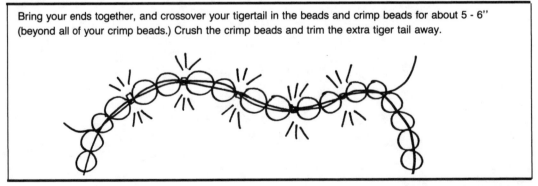

METHOD TWO: USING THREAD, BUT NOT KNOTTED BETWEEN BEADS

You'll Need:

- Silk or nylon bead cord
- One twisted wire needle
- Beads of your choice
- Scotch tape
- Cement

Step One:

Do not make any knot in the end of the thread; tape it about 5'' from the end. String all of your beads.

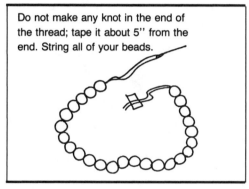

Step Two:

When you get to the end of your stringing, make a square knot with your two ends.

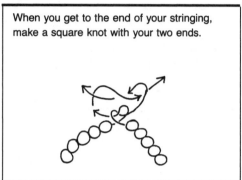

Step Three:

Run the end with the needle still attached through several beads, then make an overhand knot. Run it through a few more beads, and make another knot. Do this about three times.

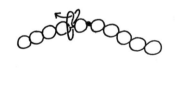

Step Four:

Now, add a needle to the other end. Again, knot every so often. Cement all of your knots. Trim your ends.

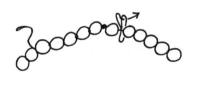

METHOD THREE: USING THREAD, AND KNOTTING BETWEEN BEADS

You'll Need:

- Silk or nylon bead cord
- One twisted wire needle
- Beads of your choice
- Scotch tape
- Cement

Step One:

Thread on three beads. Leave a 10"
tail. Do not make any knots between these
beads. After your fourth bead, you can start
knotting between the rest of the beads as usual.

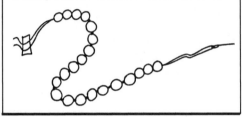

Step Two:

When you get to the last two beads, don't knot
between them. Bring your two ends together,
and make a square knot.

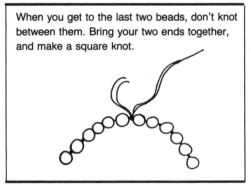

Step Three:

Bring the end with the needle through the
first bead. Make an overhand knot around your
thread.

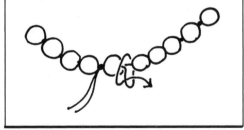

Step Four:

Add a needle to the second end and repeat.
Continue on until you have filled in all
the "knot gaps". Cement all of your "ending"
knots, and trim when dry.

Multi-Strand Necklaces

METHOD ONE: THE EASIEST WAY — MULTISTRAND CLASPS

If you can string a single strand necklace, then you can make a multistrand with this technique. The easiest way to complete a multistrand necklace is to use a clasp designed for multiple strands. This will work for necklaces strung on both tiger tail or thread.

PEARL AND FLOWER NECKLACE

Materials Needed:

- One acrylic flower center
- Two strands of 16" faux pearls
- 3 yards "F" weight silk
- 24 lavender 4mm accent beads
- One clasp that accommodates multiple strands
- Four knot covers
- Cement
- One twisted wire needle

HOW TO DO IT:

String each strand, running the thread through the back of the flower ornament.

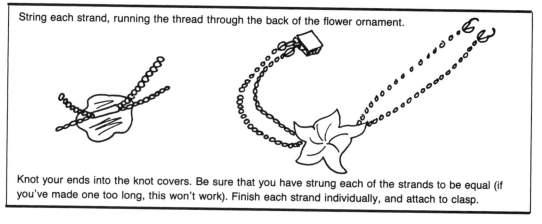

Knot your ends into the knot covers. Be sure that you have strung each of the strands to be equal (if you've made one too long, this won't work). Finish each strand individually, and attach to clasp.

METHOD TWO: GOING FROM A SINGLE TO A DOUBLE STRAND

This is almost the same as stringing a single strand, but some strands share common beads. You have to run the threads from the other strands at the bottom through all of the strands at the sides. You can end with a common knot cover.

This technique can also be used when you have three strands that feed into one common large bead at intervals.

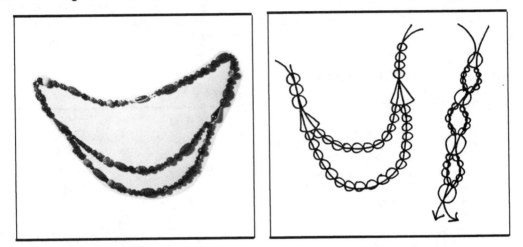

METHOD THREE: FEED ALL ENDS INTO A COMMON KNOT COVER:

This is a great solution when working with smaller beads. It's easy with fresh water pearls: just end each strand in the same knot cover (clamshells work best). This can be done in segments that attach to stations or centers, or as a continuous length of necklace.

THE BEST LITTLE BEADING BOOK

METHOD FOUR: USING END CONES

Step One:

Design your first strand. Remember, you'll be using an end cone or some other device to gather your strands at the back. It's best to put filler beads for the first 2 - 3" or so on each end. The problem of using accent beads too close to the back is that you may make it very difficult on yourself when it comes time to assemble the necklace. Make sure you leave nice, long threads (at least 6" each side) to make fastening easier. As you complete each strand, make knots in both ends, so no beads escape.

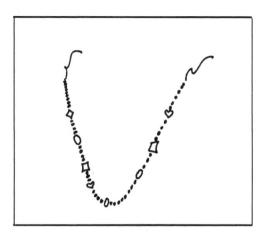

Step Two:

Lay your first strand out in a straight line. Use scotch tape and secure to a table. Build the design of your second strand by laying right next to the first. This way, you know that all of your beads won't line up in the wrong place.

For most designs, it's best if you offset your accent beads — they look better when they have that "random" feel. Build each strand off of that first one.

If you wish for all of your strands to be the same length, line the knots up evenly. If you wish to have varying lengths (a la Parisian loop or graduated lengths), then bring in the strands that you want shorter by ½ inch each side.

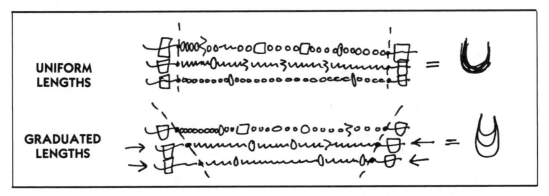

UNIFORM LENGTHS

GRADUATED LENGTHS

When Using Tiger Tail:

Step One:

String your necklace on tigertail, but instead of adding a clasp, just make a loop when you use your crimp beads. Thread these on to one eye pin.

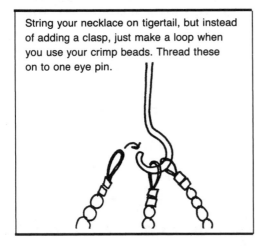

Step Two:

Using your plier, coil the eye of the eyepin to secure, so it can't pull out. Carefully crimp this with your plier.

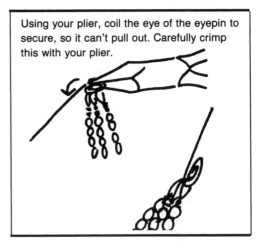

Step Three:

Slide on end cone over shaft of eyepin.

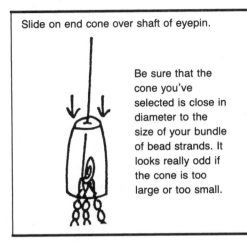

Be sure that the cone you've selected is close in diameter to the size of your bundle of bead strands. It looks really odd if the cone is too large or too small.

Step Four:

Push the cone down, and bend the shaft of the eyepin into a coil around the top top of the end cone to act like a spring. (It pushes the cone down so it can't ride up.)

When Using Thread:

Step One:

When you are stringing with a thread, it's VERY important that you leave enough extra thread to join the ends (at least 6'' each side). As already discussed, go ahead and string your multiple strands. Lay your strands together with the knots lined up. If you twist them into a bundle (like a cable) you will find that they are easier to handle. Make an overhand knot, and using your pliers, open the eye of the eyepin and insert this knotted group of ends.

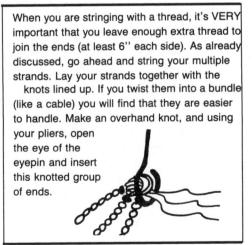

Step Two:

Using your plier, coil the eye of the eyepin to secure it so that your threads can't pull out. Crimp this carefully with your plier, as closely as possible.

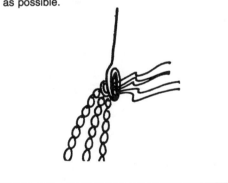

Step Three:

Using a half-hitch knot, knot the bundle of threads up the post of the eye pin for extra strength. Do this 3 - 4 times. Cement the knots from top to bottom (to where the beads begin). Cement like crazy! The more cement, the stronger it will be.

Step Four:

Slide the end cone over this nice gooey mess (the shaft of the eye pin will fit right into the little hole on the end).

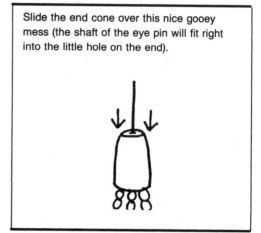

Step Five:

Coil the shaft of the eye pin around itself (this is the time to include the clasp). Do this to both sides.

METHOD FIVE: USING A BEAD IN PLACE OF AN END CONE

The dynamics work exactly the same as the previous technique, but the difference is using a bead in place of an end cone. Sometimes a bead needs to be reamed out to make the hole bigger. Needle files come in very handy for this.

METHOD SIX: USING NECKLACE BARS

This works pretty much the same as the knot cover technique, but you're attaching each strand to a necklace bar, which in turn is attached to the clasp. With this method, both tiger tail and threads work.

METHOD SEVEN: MAKING LOOPS OF BEADS

There are several ways to do this. You can make a simple loop that is caught by a separator bar. It wouldn't hurt to reinforce with several passes through the end loop, to make sure it can't pull out. This will help strengthen the entire piece. You can also combine this with Peyote or Comanche Stitches. Please see the section on Working With Seedbeads for more ideas.

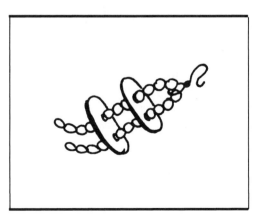

METHOD EIGHT: WEAVING SEEDBEADS TO FORM AN ENDING

It is possible to use the Comanche Stitch, Circular Comanche Stitch, Peyote Stitch, or Circular Peyote Stitch to achieve some truly wonderful results. Please see the section on Working With Seedbeads for more ideas.

METHOD NINE: USING A PEARL SHORTENER

If you string long, continuous strands of beads (36" or longer), you can group them by twisting your strands together and fastening with a pearl shortener.

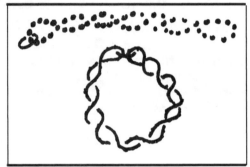

METHOD TEN: COMBINING TWO NECKLACES TO CREATE ONE

By using half-hitch knots, you can create a very dramatic effect by mixing contrasting colors. Use a different color necklace on one side, then fasten with a pearl shortener.

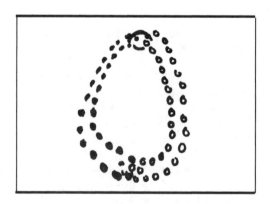

Multi-Strand Seedbead Necklace

Multi-strand necklaces are a way to take the design process one step further, adding dimensions and character that sometimes a single-strand just can't create.

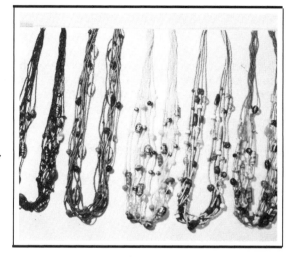

Supplies Needed:
- One hank of seedbeads
- English beading needle sized for seedbeads (either #10 or #12)
- Nymo thread in "F" weight
- Variety of accent beads
- One clasp
- Two end cones
- Two eye pins
- Cement

Step One:

Decide how long you want this necklace to be. 24" — 26" is right for most people. As discussed on page 123, measure your thread and string. Make your accent beads fall in a random pattern.

Step Two:

End each strand with a knot. Build your next strands off of the first. End as shown when working with end cones.

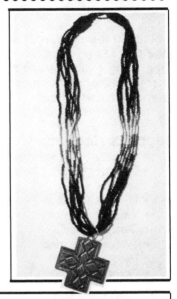

The Southwestern Seedbead Necklace

The ends of this necklace were done with the Circular Comanche Stitch. The clasp is a wooden bead that has been covered by seedbeads.

Supplies Needed:
- Black and multicolor seedbeads
- #10 English beading needle
- Nymo in "F" weight
- Fat bugle beads
- Ornament
- Cement

Step One:

String your seedbeads in the following pattern: just about all of your seedbeads are black, except for a 4" band on either side of the center. It's best if you leave a 5" band of black seedbeads in the center, so the colors won't be too far back in the necklace to show. To make your rainbow, use about 5 seedbeads of each color (brown, red, red-orange, orange, yellow, green, light blue, royal blue, violet).

Don't forget to leave nice long ends (at least one foot) for easy working of the ends.

Step Two:

Using one of your long threads, lash the large bugles together to create the base for the Comanche Stitch. One by one, use your long threads as needed to stitch. Work the Comanche Stitch until there are 3 beads left in the row.

Step Three:

Cover a wooden bead with beads (see section on Beading a Bead) and attach to your necklace. Make a buttonhole that's the right size for your wooden bead on the opposite end of the necklace.

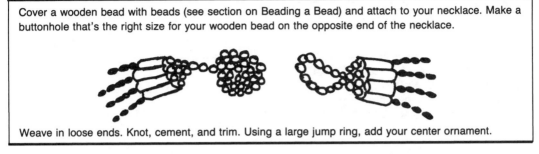

Weave in loose ends. Knot, cement, and trim. Using a large jump ring, add your center ornament.

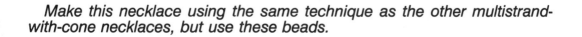

The Faux Zuni Necklace

This variation of a multi-strand necklace is patterned after the Native American necklaces that are so popular. You can make this with only turquoise chips, or you can mix several semiprecious chips.

Supplies Needed:
- "F" weight silk
- Four 16" strands of shell heishi beads
- Two 16" strands of semiprecious chips
- Two end cones
- Two eye pins
- One clasp
- Cement
- A chain nose plier

Make this necklace using the same technique as the other multistrand-with-cone necklaces, but use these beads.

Turquoise Necklace

Sometimes the problem with flat disk beads is that they don't hang right at the bottom curve and your thread shows. A good solution is to use small shell heishi in between the turquoise. This creates a gentler curve.

Supplies Needed:

- Turquoise graduated disks
- One strand of shell-heishi
- Two eye pins
- Two end cones
- Two yards "F" weight silk
- One twisted wire needle
- Cement

How To Do It:

Even though this is a single strand, the ends were attached in the same manner as a multi-strand to give it a more authentic look. String your turquoise alternately with ¼" of heishi for a smooth curve.

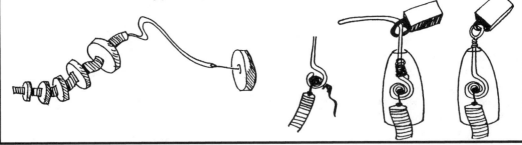

THE BEST LITTLE BEADING BOOK

Southwestern Charm Necklaces

Both of these necklaces are very easy to make, yet similar ones sell for upwards of $600 at a local department store! The technique is exactly like the Multi-Strand Seedbead Necklace, but you use 4mm beads for your filler beads, instead of seedbeads. You also add Southwestern charms to these to give them style. On the one of the left, a locket has been added. Please see pages 54 and 55 for these and other similar necklaces.

WHITE HEART/TURQUOISE NECKLACE (Left)

Supplies Needed:

- One sterling locket
- Four strands of white hearts
- Two strands of turquoise disks
- "F" weight silk thread
- Miscellaneous charms with a Southwestern flavor
- Silver jump rings
- Peruvian beads
- One 1"button for a clasp
- Two end cones (or thimbles)
- Two eye pins
- 2 knot covers

Step One:

Decide on the length of this necklace. Prepare your materials to string in the manner already shown. Continue stringing each strand, but as add the locket, string through one or two common beads so that the strand is interwoven at this centerpoint.

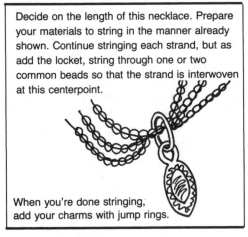

When you're done stringing, add your charms with jump rings.

Step Two:

You have the option of using a button as your clasp. When you end your coiled eyepins over your end cones, leave the loop empty. You can make a short length to hold your button/button hole that affixes to this.

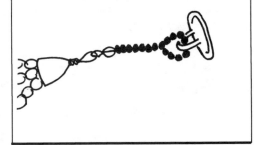

Step Three:

Thread an knot cover, then a short length of beads. Center your button in a loop of beads, and bring your needle back through the short strand of beads, and into the knot cover. Knot and cement. Attach this to each coiled eye pin.

Make the "button hole" in the same manner, but don't add the button. Be sure you make it large enough for your button to fit!

A VARIATION:

Native American bead artists use sterling thimbles instead of end cones sometimes. If you have nice thimbles you'd like to use, make a hole in the end CAREFULLY with a hammer and nail, and use in place of a cone.

These directions given also work for SOUTHWESTERN CHARM NECKLACE #2, as well as the other necklaces shown on pages 54 and 55. The main differences are in the selection of beads. To see how to incorporate the stations into the SOUTHWESTERN CHARM NECKLACE #2, please see METHOD #2 in the instructions for multi-strand stringing.

THE BEST LITTLE BEADING BOOK

Native American Collar

This collar takes almost no time to make, yet you'll get lots of compliments when you wear it! You can adjust the length to fit your neck by adding or subtracting segments.

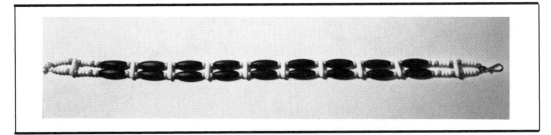

Supplies Needed:

- Eighteen red "cinnamon-glass" beads (about 1" in length).
- Forty eight light blue "E" beads
- Thirty-six white "E" beads
- Ten white glass separator bars (you can also make your own out of leather)
- "F" weight silk
- One twisted wire needle
- One hook-and-eye clasp
- Cement

Step One:

Starting at one end, thread on one strand. Pass thru one hole in each separator bar.

The end pattern is 1 blue bead, 5 white, 1 blue, 1 separator bar, 1 blue , 3 white, 1 blue, 1 white, 1 blue, *1 cinnamon, 1 blue, 1 sep bar, 1 blue, 1 cinnamon, etc., repeating from the * until you are ready for the second end, which is 1 blue, 1 white, 1 blue, 3 white, 1 blue, 1 sep bar, 1 blue, 5 white, 1 blue.

Step Two

When you get to the end, thread on one end
of the clasp (centered on end piece), and string
the second strand, passing thru the second hole
of the separator bars as you go. Be sure your
design lines up properly.

Step Three:

When you're back at the beginning, thread on
the other end of the clasp. Bring your two ends
of thread together, and knot as you would for a
continuous necklace. Crisscross the thread thru
both sides (see Continuous Necklaces), cement
and trim.

NOTES:

_____

_____

_____

_____

_____

_____

_____

_____

African Ashanti Necklace

Ashantis are small cast-bronze figures from Africa which are usually found in the shapes of masks, people, and animals. As each one is made by a method called "lost-wax" casting, they are each unique because the mold is broken when they are made. Each one has great personality, and they add a very nice design element to your jewelry. The necklace here is rhodonite with brass heishi.

Supplies Needed:

- Four strands of rhodonite beads (rounds and nuggets)
- Miscellaneous rhodonite beads in shapes (leaves, larger rounds, etc.)
- Three Ashantis
- One strand brass heishi
- Two large wooden beads
- Two large brass beads
- Two eye pins
- One clasp
- One needle file with a fine tip
- Chain nose pliers

Step One:

You'll string as you would the other Multi-Strand necklaces, positioning the Ashantis at the center. Use your heishi as accent wherever you like.

Step Two:

With a needle file, ream out the wooden beads to accommodate your eye pins.

Step Three

Finish the necklace in the same manner as if you were using end cones. After affixing and cementing your threads to your eyepin, bring the shaft of the eyepin up through first the wooden bead, then the brass bead. Coil and finish.

THE BEST LITTLE BEADING BOOK

Garnet & Citrine Collar

This one takes the design process one step further. The style is a little different: here you're not only concerned with the linear design, but also with the parallel design (how the strands line up). It's important to allow yourself the trial-and-error approach when stringing this — you may get three beads beyond a certain point, yet decide you don't like the way this lines up. It's okay to "back up" to adjust.

Supplies Needed:

- One centerpiece with multiple channels for stringing
- Two strands of 4mm garnet
- Two strands of teardrop-shaped citrine beads
- Two separator bars
- Eighteen silver accent beads
- One twisted wire needle
- "F" weight silk
- Two end cones
- Two eye pins
- One clasp
- One twisted wire needle
- Cement

Step One:

It's best to layout your design before you start. Lay the strands of bead on paper, and see how they line up. It doesn't hurt to sketch a "pattern" to work by.

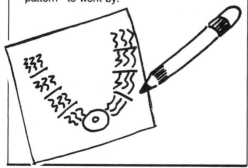

Step Two:

You're still stringing like a basic multistrand necklace, but keeping a closer eye on the overall design. Position your centerpiece; make sure your design lines up. One bead can make the difference!

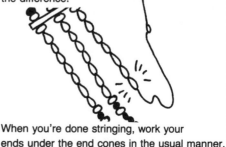

When you're done stringing, work your ends under the end cones in the usual manner.

Amethyst & Pearl Collar

This very elegant collar is perfect for New Years parties or other special occasions. It's five strands, and the lining up of the design is tricky, but well-worth it. One of the unusual elements of design is in the separator bars, which are actually purple glass two-hole buttons. When I was putting this together, I couldn't find a purple glass sep bar. I was in a fabric store and saw these buttons and fell in love! Sometimes the elements we find by accident are the best thing that could happen.

Supplies Needed:

- Two strands of 8mm amethyst firepolished crystal
- Two strands of 10mm amethyst firepolished crystal
- Twenty-four 4mm amethyst firepolished crystal
- Two strands of 6mm faux pearls
- Twenty-six 6mm rhinestone rondells
- Ten knot covers
- Five twisted wire needles
- "F" weight silk
- Sixteen 2-hole separator bars OR flat buttons (these should look like sep bars)
- One very fancy clasp
- Six jump rings

Step One:

You may want to make a paper pattern of yourself to work by before you start. The more strands in a collar the more critical the fit. If you have the bodice section of a dress pattern (or a pattern of a "yoke"), you can use these to help you lay out your design. This necklace will fit everyone a little differently. If you own a dressform, you might think about composing this necklace on it, and pinning as you work (instead of tape). Thread all five needles on 5 lengths of silk (each one is appx. 1½ yards long). Thread on your 5 knot covers (one to a strand). You'll work all 5 strands at one time, for the best accuracy. Tape them down side by side.

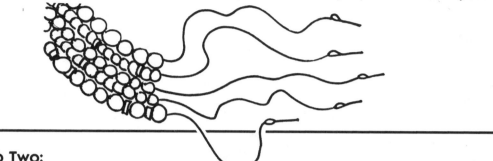

Step Two:

It's very important to note that no two necklaces will be identical because of the exact fit. Variations are caused by neck size, protruding collar bones, etc. I suggest that you play with the curve to see what you like: this project requires more creativity. Page 51 shows a larger color photo for you to follow my pattern exactly if you wish, or you can design variations of this that fit you. Don't forget to incorporate your separator bars as you work, to give this collar structure.

When you are done stringing, end your five strands in five knotcovers. Be careful that they are remained parallel the entire time, and not crossed. Cement, close knot covers, and attach to the clasp with jumprings. It's best if your clasp will accommodate at least 3 strands (you can double up on the outer ones).

MATCHING EARRINGS:

Supplies:

- Two teardrop side-drilled amethyst crystal
- Two 8mm round amethyst crystal
- Two 6mm pearls
- Four 6mm rhinestone rondells
- Two earwires
- 24 gauge wire

HOW TO DO IT:

Center the teardrop crystal on a 4'' piece of wire. Bring up the ends together thru the other beads. Twist and coil at the top, interlocking with your earwires.

NOTES:

_____

_____

_____

_____

_____

_____

THE BEST LITTLE BEADING BOOK

Needlewoven Charm Bracelet

If you enjoy hand-sewing, you'll love this project. Basically, it's just stitching a figure-8 (like Soutache-cord) and embellishing it with beads as you go. Give it personal meaning, using charms, old gum machine toys, buttons, and other personal momentos. It's fun to have a theme when you do this project. It's very important to work as tightly as possible as you stitch. This bracelet takes about two hours to complete.

Supplies Needed:

- One stiff needle (tapistry, embroidery, or needlepoint needle is recommended) for stitching
- Two twisted wire needles (to use when adding beads)
- One button, about 1" in size (buttons with a shank work best), to be used as your clasp.
- Lots of beads, charms, etc. (odds and ends are great)
- One spool of "F" weight silk thread. Because stitching styles differ, it's impossible to predict how much thread is needed. After you have made one of these, you'll be better acquainted with your own style. I recommend that you DON'T use white, because it will show dirt and wear. Choose a vibrant color that fits in with your color scheme.
- One clipboard for gripping the bracelet as you work
- Scotch tape

Step One:

Cut ten lengths of silk thread, each one is one yard long. Cut an 11th piece, this one is two yards long. Fold over the bundle of ten threads, and, using the long 11th thread, tie the bundle together with a square knot.

Step Two:

You now have 20 strands of thread (the ten folded over) that form your core. The 11th thread is used for stitching. You are starting at the button hole side. The loop should be close to the size of your button. The size of this loop will shift as you stitch, so you will need to adjust it every so often.

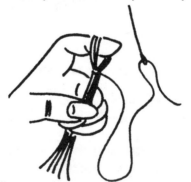

Thread your stiff needle with the long piece of the 11th strand. The short tail can be joined with the core bundle of threads. Holding this in your left hand (as shown)*, stitch through the knot a couple of times to help secure the size. Remember, you can make this buttonhole smaller if needed by stitching, but you CAN'T cut it to make it larger.

THE BEST LITTLE BEADING BOOK

Step Three:

You're working single thread, in a figure-eight stitch. DO NOT stitch the loop closed — it needs to remain open. You will work by stitching through the center of the bundle, alternating right and left (like a buttonhole stitch. Work up the side of the buttonhole. Stitch tightly, and keep your stitches uniform. Continue working all the way around. When you've completed the buttonhole, you're ready to start the main part of the bracelet.

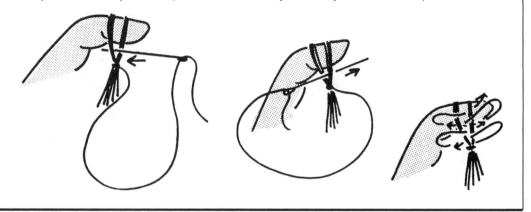

Step Four:

Clip the button-hole section to your clipboard. Stitch in your figure-8 for about ¼'' more. You are now ready TO add beads. Pull off two strands from your core thread. Thread your twisted wire needle on them, and string on one bead. Remove the needle, and tape these two threads with the bead on them to the clipboard, separate from the remaining bundle. Continue stitching, pulling off other strands (in groups of two) and adding beads or charms, taping them away from the group.

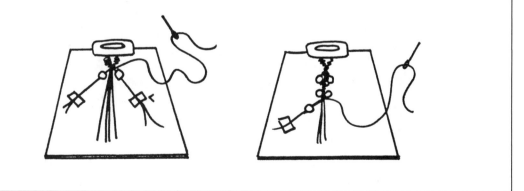

Step Five:

As you weave to the bottom of each bead, weave those strands back into the center bundle. Remember to add your beads at different intervals, so it has a fuller look to it.

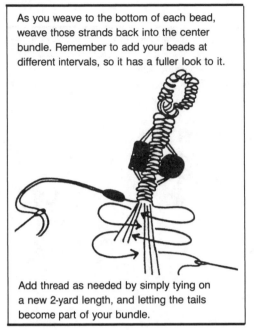

Add thread as needed by simply tying on a new 2-yard length, and letting the tails become part of your bundle.

Step Six:

When you are 1/2'' from the desired length, divide your core threads in half, and cut half of them off at an angle. This is so there is no bulge when you weave your ends together.

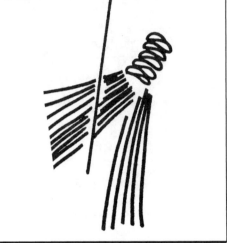

Step Seven:

Thread a button onto your remaining long core threads. Fold them over, and stitch them securely.

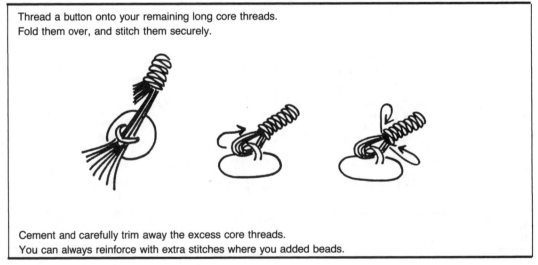

Cement and carefully trim away the excess core threads. You can always reinforce with extra stitches where you added beads.

Needlewoven Charm Necklace

Now that you've mastered the bracelet, are you ready for a matching necklace? The basic technique is the same as the previous project, the Needlewoven Charm Bracelet. The only differences are in the measurements.

You'll be using the exact same materials, but cutting longer lengths of silk thread. For the necklace, you need **20** lengths of silk thread, each one **2** yards long. Your 21st thread, used for stitching, will still be a comfortable length for you to work with.

Please be aware that this necklace should be fuller than the bracelet (that's why we doubled the number of core threads). You'll need more beads and embellishments to give it a full look. Your finished necklace can be any length you desire. There's lots of room for creative expression with this project!

Please see page 59 for full color photo.

Woven Crystal Bracelet

This bracelet is quick, stunning, and inexpensive. It's 7¼" long, and has 9 repeating segments. Measure your wrist and make any adjustments accordingly by adding or subtracting segments.

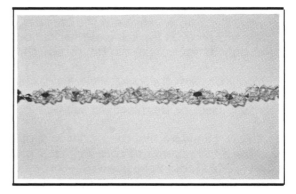

Supplies Needed:

- 72 AB (Aurora Borealis) crystal beads, 3½ - 4 mm in size.
- 9 4mm accent crystals (all the same color, or multi-colored)
- 2 knot covers
- 1 clasp
- 10' of "F" weight silk thread
- 1 twisted wire needle.

Step One:

Cut 3' of silk. Thread your needle; you're working double thread. Make a knot in the ends, and add a knot cover. Add two AB crystal, one accent crystal, then two more AB.

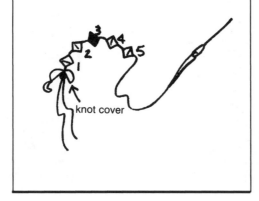

knot cover

Step Two:

Now, weaving in a circular motion, bring your needle through the first three beads again, in the same direction as before.

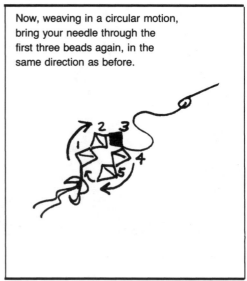

Step Three:

Add four more AB crystal, weave thru the accent crystal again, and back thru two of these latest additions.

You've made one segment of the bracelet. It's basically a figure "8", and a diamond shape. Make a knot at this point.

Step Four:

Working as tightly as possible, reinforce if necessary. Your thread should not be loose and "floppy". Repeat segment, adding 2 AB crystal, accent crystal, 2 more AB crystal, and so on.

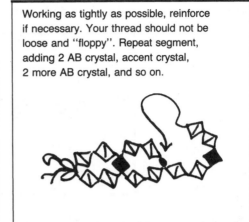

Step Five:

Repeat as many times as necessary for length. Secure second side with knot cover.

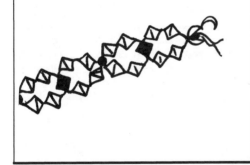

Step Six:

Cement knots, close knot covers, and add clasp.

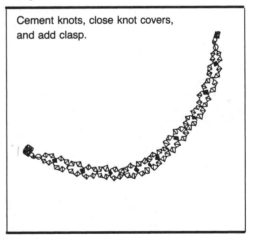

Double Strand Woven Bracelet

This takes the previous project out one step further, to a double strand.

Supplies Needed:

- 126 dark green 3x5mm crystal beads
- Eighteen red 3x5mm crystal beads
- Four knot covers
- One clasp made for two strands
- 20' of "F" weight silk thread
- 1 twisted wire needle.
- Cement

How To Do It:

Do the previous project as shown, using your red crystal beads as your accents. Now, thread a second needle, string on a new knot cover, add 2 green crystal beads, one red, and thread thru one existing green crystal in your bracelet, and add one green. That makes one round. Thread thru the same first 2 green and red, then up thru the existing green, add 3 more green. Working in the same direction, go thru that last red, the existing green, and the first green one you just added. That's loop number two. Continue on (your direction of stitching is like a figure-8).

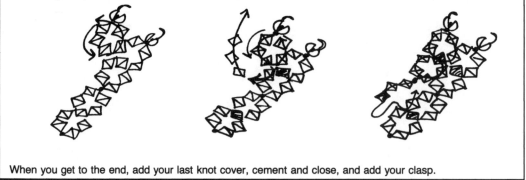

When you get to the end, add your last knot cover, cement and close, and add your clasp.

Pink Crystal Necklace

This is barely a weave, and it comes together so quickly, yet looks so elegant.

Supplies Needed:

- 132 6mm pink diamond-shaped crystal
- 11 8x10mm rectangular side drilled crystal
- 2 knot covers
- 1 clasp
- 3 teardrop sidedrilled crystal
- 4 yards "F" weight silk
- 1 twisted wire needle
- Cement

For matching earrings:

- Two 8mm diamond-shaped crystal
- Two teardrop sidedrilled crystal
- Twelve 4mm diamond-shaped crystal
- Two earwires
- Two knot covers

Step One:

Thread your needle with ½ yards of thread. You'll work with your thread doubled. Make a knot with both ends, and thead on the knot cover. You'll first string the inner strand.

The pattern is: 23 6mm crystal, one rectangle,
2 6mm crystal, 1 rectangle, 2 6mm crystal, 1 rectangle,
2 6mm crystal, 1 rectangle, 2 6mm crystal, 1 rectangle,
2 6mm crystal, 1 rectangle, 2 6mm crystal, 1 rectangle,
2 6mm crystal, 1 rectangle, 2 6mm crystal, 1 rectangle,
2 6mm crystal, 1 rectangle, 2 6mm crystal, 1 rectangle, 23 6mm crystal.
End with the second knot cover, and make a knot inside to end it. Slip the needle off the thread, but DO NOT CUT ANYTHING!

Step Two:

Now, Thread the needle again with another 1½ yards of thread. Go into the same knot cover that you started with, and thread up into the first ten crystal beads. Add fifteen new 6mm crystal beads, and thread through the first rectangle bead. Add seven 6mm crystal, then go through the next rectangle bead.

Add six 6mm crystal, then one teardrop, then four 6mm crystal, then through the next rectangle bead. Add 6mm crystal, one teardrop, four 6mm crystal, the next rectangle bead. Again, four 6mm crystal, one teardrop, four 6mm crystal, the next rectangle bead. Add seven 6mm crystal, the next rectangle bead, fifteen 6mm crystal, and thread back through the last ten 6mm crystal on the first strand.

Step Three:

Go through your last knot cover. Make 2 square knots inside each knot cover, and cement. Close the knot covers and trim the excess thread. Attach the clasp to the knot covers.

THE MATCHING EARRINGS:

Thread the remaining silk thread onto your poor, tired needle. Work double thread. Thread on a knot cover, add the large 8mm crystal, then three 4mm crystal, a teardrop, three 4mm crystal, and close the loop by going back up through the large 8mm crystal and back up into the knot cover. Square knot your thread, cement, and close the knot cover. Trim the excess thread, and make your second earring.

Red & Clear Crystal Collar

You'll enjoy making this necklace because it goes so quickly!

Supplies Needed:

- 290 4mm crystal beads
- Thirty 6mm red crystal beads
- Eight 8mm red crystal beads
- Forty-eight 10mm red crystal beads
- Four knot covers
- One clasp for a two-strand necklace
- 10' of "F" weight silk thread
- 1 twisted wire needle.
- Thirty seven eye pins

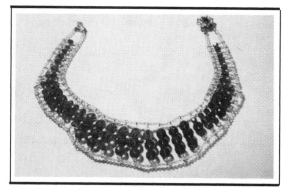

- One chain nose plier
- Cement

Step One:

You'll first thread your eyepins with combinations of red and clear crystal. You'll make short segments of varying lengths, then close the loops (as if you were making an earring).

You need six with one crystal, one 4mm red, and one crystal;

Four with one crystal, one 6mm red, and one crystal.

Two with one crystal, one 8mm red, and one crystal.

Two with one crystal, two 4mm red, one crystal.

Four with one crystal, three 4mm red, one crystal.

Two with one crystal, two 10mm red, one crystal.

Four with one crystal, one 4mm red, one 8mm red, one 4mm red, one crystal.

Nine with one crystal, three 10mm red, one crystal.

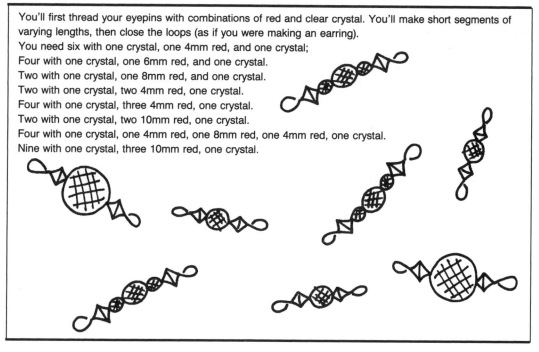

Step Two:

Lay them all out in order of size, with the longest ones in the middle, tapering toward the ends. Thread your needle with 1½ yards of thread, doubled. Add a knot cover, and start stringing. Start with five 4mm crystal, then one eyepin (shortest), then two 4mm crystal, one more eyepin, etc. Add your eyepins intermittently with the remainder of the 4mm crystal. You'll have to be aware of the shape, so you may find that sometimes two 4mm crystal works between, sometimes three or four. Finish the one strand with a knot cover.

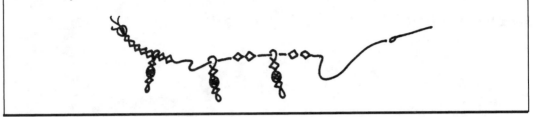

Step Three:

Cut new thread, add a knot cover, and string your second strand, catching the other loop of the eyepins where they fall in the design.

Finish the second strand with a knot cover, cement, and join to the clasp.

THE BEST LITTLE BEADING BOOK

Woven Crystal Collar

You can build this collar to be as full as you'd like. There are two main parts of the design. The collar works if you end it after the first part, or you can continue on through the second part to make a REALLY stunning piece. The photo on page 58 shows the fire in the AB crystal.

Supplies Needed:

- 156 6mm diamond-shaped AB crystal
- Thirty-three flat 10mm AB crystal
- Fifty-four round 6mm AB crystal
- Twenty-six 8mm round AB crystal
- One fancy clasp that takes two strands
- Four knot covers
- "F" weight silk
- Two twisted wire needles
- Cement

Step One:

Thread each needle with 4 yards of thread. Working with your thread doubled, add a knot cover to each strand. Make a knot outside each, and add 2 of the 6mm diamond shaped crystal to each.

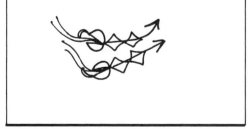

Step Two:

Take your large 10mm flat crystal, and criss-cross the two strands by running the needles thru in opposite directions. Now add 2 more 6mm diamond crystal to each strand, and again criss-cross threads inside a 10mm crystal. Repeat this pattern until all of the 10mm crystal are used. End each strand to match the beginning. Add your 2 other knot covers, BUT DO NOT CLOSE THEM.

This makes a dandy collar just to here if you like.

Step Three:

Now, thread your needle again with 2 yards of silk (again your thread is doubled). Make a knot in one of the knot covers, and weave through the bottom of your existing crystal 'til you are ⅓ of the way across.

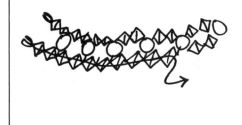

Step Four:

Start making loops of crystal (1 6mm round, 1 8mm round, 1 6mm round, skipping 2 of the diamond shaped ones with each loop. Continue across the row, ending when you are ⅔ of the way across the collar.

Step Five:

Now turn, and work the next row like the previous, but offset the loops. Complete the row.

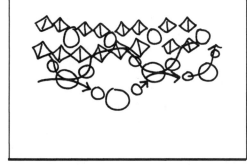

Step Six:

Row three is also offset from the previous row, but now you're stringing 2 round 6mm, 1 round 8mm, 2 round 6mm in each loop. Each row tapers in just a bit, as the loops are offset.

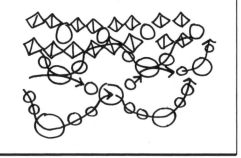

THE BEST LITTLE BEADING BOOK

Step Seven:

The last row consists of 5 loops, with the pattern of 2 6mm diamond crystal, 1 8mm round, 2 6mm diamond in each loop. Finish the row, weave through the beads to get back to the knot cover. Now, cement and close your knot covers. Add your clasp.

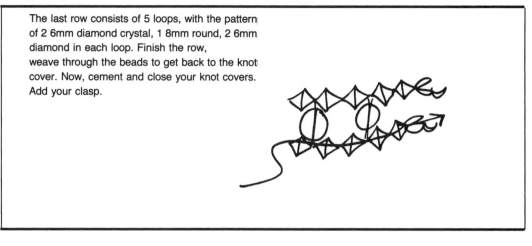

Woven Semiprecious Necklace

People always comment when I wear this necklace. It looks very hard, but it's actually very easy to make. Here are two variations.

AMETHYST & BLUE LACE NECKLACE

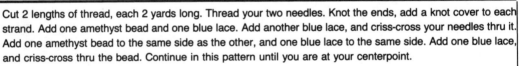

Supplies Needed:

- 191 4mm blue lace agate beads
- 149 4mm amethyst beads
- Six knot covers
- 1 clasp that takes 3 strands
- "F" weight silk thread
- Two twisted wire needles
- Cement
- Tape

Step One:

Cut 2 lengths of thread, each 2 yards long. Thread your two needles. Knot the ends, add a knot cover to each strand. Add one amethyst bead and one blue lace. Add another blue lace, and criss-cross your needles thru it. Add one amethyst bead to the same side as the other, and one blue lace to the same side. Add one blue lace, and criss-cross thru the bead. Continue in this pattern until you are at your centerpoint.

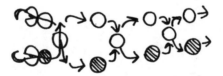

Step Two:

Holding this so that the amethysts are on the right side, with your left needle, add 3 blue lace. Bring your left needle around in a circular motion, thru the 3 beads you just added. Bring your other needle thru that third bead (criss-cross threads in this bead). Now you have made the V-shape in the front. Continue on to be even with the first half. When completed, add the knot covers, but DON'T CLOSE THEM.

Step Three:

Cut 2 new threads. Thread your needles. Make knots in the ends, and add a new knot cover to one strand, and go into the existing knot cover away from the amethyst side. Using the same technique, you'll continue weaving, but weave into the existing necklace instead of adding a new blue lace (keep adding amethyst).

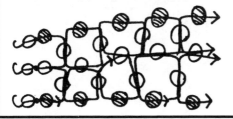

Step Four:

When you get to the "V" shape, you'll add extra beads to adjust so that it lays flat.

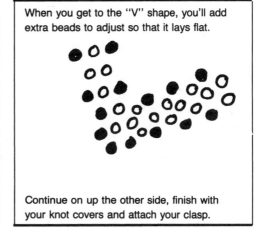

Continue on up the other side, finish with your knot covers and attach your clasp.

The ROSE QUARTZ AND GARNET version also pictured is actually a lot easier to make — there's no real pattern to follow. You might want to sketch out other combinations of stones — this design looks very different when you use a variety of beads.

Watchbands

Making a beaded watchband is fun and easy. There are so many styles to choose from, no two ever look alike. When making a watchband, the first thing you want to do is measure your wrist. The average wrist is 7". Yours may be larger or smaller. Most watches that have fixed-length bands come in 6¾, 7¾, and 8¼ sizes. It's best to have an idea which size will work for you, as many of these bands do not adjust their length.

The natural tendency is to make the watchband too large. It's a good idea to measure first, using the following method:

$$
\begin{array}{rl}
7" & \text{(Size of wrist)} \\
-\ 1" & \text{(Length of watch — from springbar to springbar)} \\
\hline
6" & \text{Length of band that you will bead.}
\end{array}
$$

You will divide that final length into 2 equal sections. In this case, that is 3" each.

Every watchband you do will differ slightly, as some watches are different sizes and may attach differently.

The Southwest Watchband

One of the most popular watchbands right now is the "Southwest Watchband". Made of odds and ends of beads, it costs almost nothing to make, yet sells for hundreds of dollars in fine department stores! You can make this watchband for under twenty dollars.

Supplies Needed:

- 1 watch
- Misc. beads — mainly semi-precious, like turquoise or amethyst; but also chevrons, glass, brass heishi, and other rustic looking beads.
- Antique-look button for clasp
- 8-10 yards of "F" weight silk thread
- Bullion (French coil)
- 1 needle
- 2 pony beads
- Jewelers' cement
- 24 gauge wire and 1 wooden skewer OR Watchband enhancer (optional)
- Chain nose plier

Step One:

Start by cutting off 2 feet of silk. You'll work with the thread doubled. Do NOT make a knot in the end of this thread.

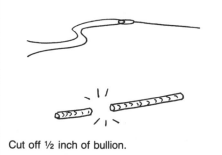

Cut off ½ inch of bullion.

Step Two:

Bring your needle through the first bead, then the bullion. Bend the bullion in half, and make knot in the thread just outside the ends of the bullion.

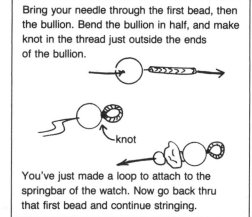

knot

You've just made a loop to attach to the springbar of the watch. Now go back thru that first bead and continue stringing.

Step Three:

When you've beaded 2½", bring your thread thru one pony bead. Make a small loop. Center your button on this loop, and pass the thread back thru the pony bead. You should make a knot at this point.

knot

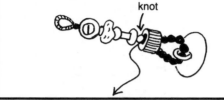

Step Four:

Continue 'til the second half matches the first. End with the bullion in the same way. (make loop, knot, back through the first bead).

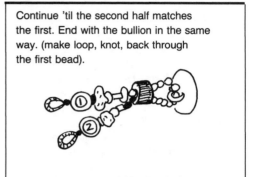

Step Five:

If you desire a third strand, cut another length of thread, anchor end with bullion, and work the same as before.

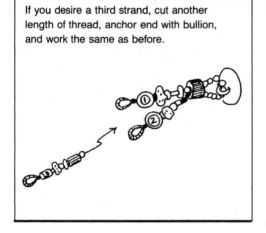

Step Six:

When you get to the pony bead, wrap the thread several times around the other two strands (inside pony bead), knot and end.

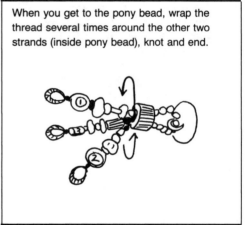

Step Seven:

Complete the other side of the band,
but this time, your loop is a button hole,
and should fit your button.
When you are done, cement all knots.

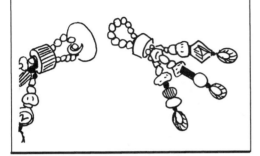

Step Eight:

You're now ready to attach your band to
your watch. Slip the springbar through
the loops you've made with your bullion.

Step Nine:

Or, you can take 24 gauge wire and wrap a coil around a wooden skewer.
This is the same size as most springbars. Cut even lengths to act as spacers between
your strands, so they don't "flop around".

A Nice Variation:

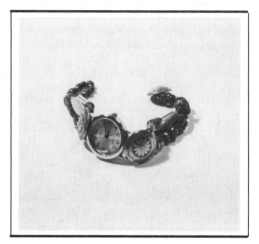

For an nice accent, add watch enhancers. These look like conchos, and just slip right over the loops to cover them up.

The Woven Watchband

Using the weaving stitch shown on page 158, you can weave a beautiful watchband. Try it with semiprecious beads (these are hematite), or with crystal.

Supplies Needed:
- One watch face
- Three strands of 4mm hematite beads
- One bracelet clasp
- Four knot covers
- Cement
- One twisted wire needle
- "F" weight silk thread

See page 158 for the instructions for this stitch. When you're done stringing, attach your knot covers to the spring bars and the clasp.

The Twenty Minute Watchband

This is the quickest, easiest watchband in the world! Strung on elastic and fastened with wire, it looks so great, no one would guess it was this easy!

Supplies Needed:
- One watch face
- ½ yard ¼"-thick elastic
- Assortment of trade beads, pony beads, etc.
- 24 gauge wire
- One chain nose plier
- Two watch enhancers (optional)

Step One:

Cut the elastic in half. Make a loop and secure by winding the wire very tightly around it. String on your beads.

Step Two:

Make a loop in the other end, and secure with wire. Make two strands in this manner. Pull tightly as you secure so that it will not be too loose on you.

Attach the loops to the springbars. Use the enhancers to hide the ends, if you like.

Bent Wire Watchband

Crystal and marcasite combine to make this an elegant watch for evening.

Supplies Needed:
- One watch face
- 20 gauge wire
- Twelve crystal beads
- Two 3-hole rhinestone separator bars
- Two necklace bars
- One clasp

How To Do It:

Simply link the wire (as shown in the section on Wire Bending) to form a "chain" look. Attach your clasp when done.

The "Bubbly" Watchband

Worked on chain, this one takes a little longer because of all the segments on head pins. However, it's worth the work.

Supplies Needed:
- One watch face
- Many odds and ends of beads
- Many head pins
- A bracelet clasp
- An 18" length of curb chain
- Jump rings
- Chain nose pliers

Step One:

Make ten zillion little head pins with beads on them (just like earrings). Cut your chain into 3" lengths, and connect with the jump rings at both ends.

Attach the beaded headpins to your chains, one at a time.

Step Two:

When you're done, attach the clasp to one side of the jump ring, and the watchface to the other.

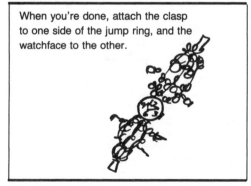

The Peyote Stitch Watchband

If you like the Peyote Stitch, you'll love this watchband.

Supplies Needed:
- 11° hex or tile beads in 3 colors
- Nymo "B" weight
- #10 English beading needle
- Cement
- One watch face

Step One:

Cut 1 yard of nymo. Thread your needle. You're working simgle thread. See section on Peyote Stitch for the exact steps to this stitch. Start at the point. String on 3 beads. Gradually widen to 8 wide.

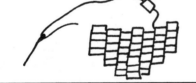

Step Two:

You outside beads will remain the base color. Your inside beads will change in this pattern:

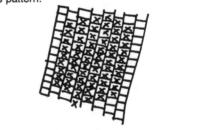

Step Three:

Your accent colors will alternate. Keep working until you have the length you need. This band is worked in all one piece.

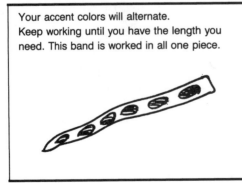

Step Four:

Attach a small buckle or clasp to this last end (weave it in). End your threads and cement.

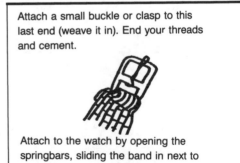

Attach to the watch by opening the springbars, sliding the band in next to the watch, then putting the springbars back.

THE BEST LITTLE BEADING BOOK

Beading on Fabric

This is a nice skill to have. You can make your own beaded dresses or vests; you can cover a fabric box in beads. Just about everyone has sewn: adding beads is just the next step.

When you bead on fabric, you usually work single thread, unless the beads are quite large and need to be reinforced.

There are several methods for beading on fabric. You may want to modify these, or work in a combination of them.

THE THREE-BEAD METHOD

This method gives a lot of control with the placement of your beads. It's perfect for solid bead coverage.

Step One:

Draw out your design on your cloth. Cement your cabochon into position with "527". Place the cloth in the embroidery hoop, thread the needle; knot the end. Stitch thru the cloth to the right side.

Step Two:

With the 3-bead method, you will add 3 beads at a time. After picking up 3 beads, bring the needle thru the cloth.

Step Three:

Bring up the needle just before the third bead. Go thru that bead in the same direction as you're working. Now add 3 more beads and repeat.

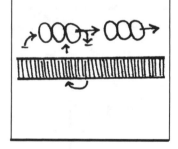

COUCHING / ONE & TWO NEEDLE METHODS

One Needle:

After you stitch, you circle back and tack down your stitches.

Two Needle:

The first needle strings the beads in one long strand. The second one catches the first thread to tack it down every so often.

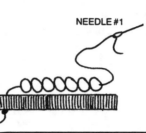

NEEDLE #1

Step Two:

Many dresses are beaded in this method, because intricate designs can be achieved. however, it's just not practical for solid bead coverage. It's also very weak.

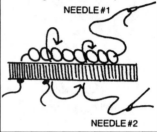

NEEDLE #1

NEEDLE #2

THE CONTINENTAL STITCH

Just like in needlepoint, but add a bead with each stitch.

Step One:

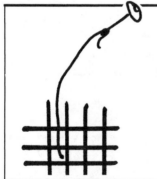

Step Two:

Step Three:

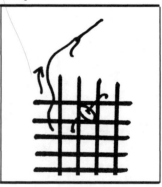

THE SATIN STITCH

This is the easiest stitch, and the quickest for covering large areas of fabric quickly.

Step One:

String 2'' of beads on your thread.

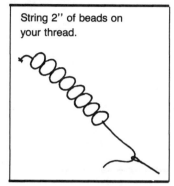

Step Two:

Pass the needle thru the cloth. Repeat again, parallel to the first row.

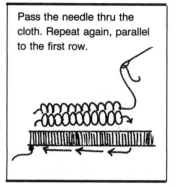

Step Three:

These stitches are loose. You can "couch" them randomly when done.

STITCHING A ROSETTE

These circular patterns sometimes have cabochons in the center, sometimes just circular designs of beads.

Step One:

If you would like to make a pattern, it's best to draw it first so you have a design to work from.

Step Two:

Lay out your main beads in 4 rows. The holes need to be facing sideways, not the center. Work outward, tacking each bead in line.

Step Three:

Fill in with the Three Bead Stitch.

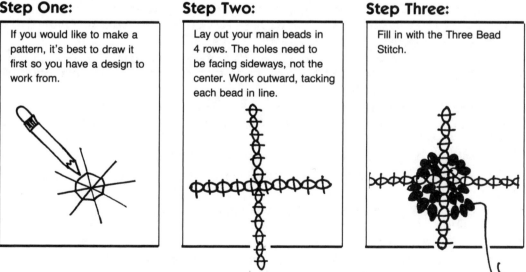

THE WHIPSTITCH

Let your thread run over the edge, stitching in a circular pattern.

STAYSTITCH:

Also known as a TACKING STITCH. Stitch in place a couple of times to hold.

RUNNING STITCH:

Same as BASTING STITCH.

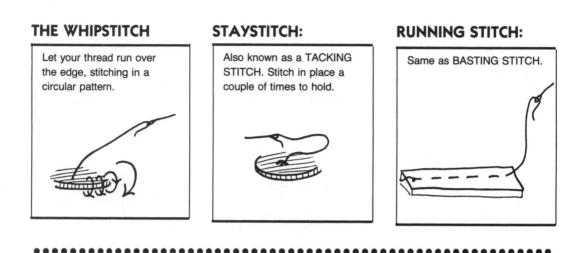

Machine Beading

Yes, you can bead on your sewing machine! You have to detach the foot and work slowly, but you can make a necklace or earrings very quickly. With this technique, you can make a multistrand necklace in under one hour.

At an art supply store, you can purchase "break-away" paper, designed to tear easily (also try watercolor papers, home-made papers, and even some brands of paper towel can be stitched through).

Stitch your beads one at a time. It takes a bead with a large hole (for the needle to pass through). Some larger seedbeads will work (as long as the needle can go through the bead easily, any bead will work).

Stitch right onto the paper and reinforce. Make it as full as you like.

When you are done, soak the paper in water to soften, and then it will tear away easily.

If you like to do Passamenterie work, you could actually stitch rattail to the paper in a configuration, then stitch beads across. When the paper is broken away, it leaves a wonderful lacy applique.

Experiment with other papers, fabric stiffener, etc. When we were kids, we would stitch beads onto burlap, then pull the threads out one at a time, and be left with just The stitched beads.

Beaded Brooch

You can combine cabochons and seedbeads to make a very unusual brooch. The seedbeads in this piece are Charlottes. They really catch the light. This same method would also work for a hair barette.

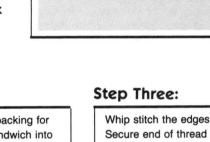

Supplies Needed:
- Five cabochons
- Charlotte beads
- Nymo in "0" weight
- Two pieces of leather for front & back
- Pin back
- Crafter's glue

Step One:

I used the Three Bead Method. When you're done stitching, CAREFULLY cut out your design. Cut the second piece of leather to the same size as the beaded piece.

Step Two:

Cut slits in the backing for the pinback. Sandwich into position, and glue the layers together. Pull tightly for a smooth fit. Glue on your cabochons

BACK

Step Three:

Whip stitch the edges to seal. Secure end of thread by stay-stitching into leather under beads.

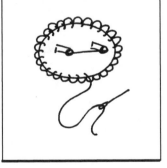

Medallon Necklace

This uses the same technique as the previous project.

Supplies Needed:
- One large cabochon or geode slice
- Seedbeads
- Nymo in "0" weight
- Sharps #7 Needle
- English Beading Needle
- Leather for backing
- Accent beads
- One piece of thin cardboard
- Crafter's glue

HOW TO DO IT:

Work exactly like the preceding project. String a multi-strand seedbead necklace and stitch into the edge of the leather under the beads. Staystitch to strengthen. Sandwich the cardboard between the front beaded piece and a backing piece of leather. Glue and whipstitch with beads shut. Work with lots of beads for fullness.

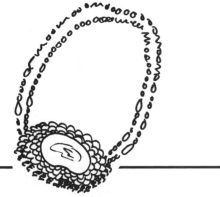

Please see page 61 for full color photo

THE BEST LITTLE BEADING BOOK

Fantasy Necklace

Marvelous for weddings or special occasions, this glorious mixture of silk flowers and beads is a real eye catcher. Several years ago, I had great success with making these necklaces for weddings. I made them in white for the brides, and the wedding colors for the bridesmaids.

Supplies Needed:
- Silk flowers in coordinating colors
- One metal or leather necklace form (kidney shaped, approximately 4" across, with 1 hole at each end)
- Seedbeads that coordinate with the flowers
- Four knot covers
- Odds and ends of crystal, glass, and semiprecious beads
- Nymo "F" weight
- Aida cloth (a 3" by 5" piece is plenty)
- #10 English beading needles
- Hot glue gun
- Jeweler's cement
- A clasp

Step One:

Foldover the aida cloth. You'll be stitching a beaded fringe into the folded edge. Start from the center. As you complete each fringe, work in a little stay-stitch to hold it. Keep going until you have fringe 3-4" wide.

Step Two:

Now you are ready to assemble the main part of the necklace. With a hot glue gun, affix the fringed beads to the metal frame.

Step Three:

Make short beaded lengths that are ended with knot covers at each end. Attach one end to the clasp, and the other to the metal piece. Cement your knots in the knot covers with the cement.

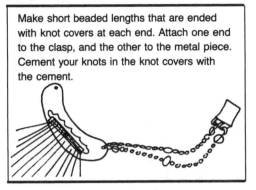

Step Four:

Arrange the flowers and glue gun them over the base of the fringe/aida cloth.

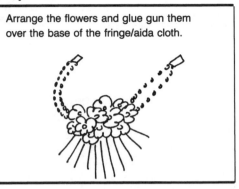

Zucchini Necklace

This necklace gets its name from another similar necklace I used to make years ago. The other was very much like this, but a lot fuller. My daughter called them Zucchini Necklaces, because they had large "whipped" knots on the side that resembled a zucchini. The name stuck. This one is a lighter, more wearable version, and I've seen them sold in boutiques for $95 — you can make this for less than $5!

Supplies Needed:
- One-yard lengths of suede, rat tail, satiny yarns, leather, or cording
- Large "macrame" beads
- Ceramic beads
- Two end cones
- Two eye pins
- Cement

Step One:

Center a bead on cord, and overhand knot
each side. Randomly offset your beads as you
add them, and tying the cords together. You
don't need many beads - it's better airy.

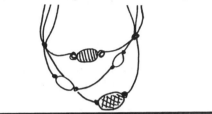

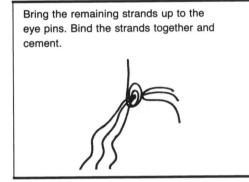

Step Two:

Combine about 10 strands, then overhand
knot them all together. You may choose to
cover or enhance this knot with a bead. Cement
the knot, and trim away all but 3 or 4 strands.

Step Three:

Bring the remaining strands up to the
eye pins. Bind the strands together and
cement.

Step Four:

End under an end cone.

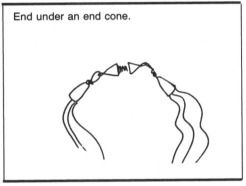

Working with Leather

It's very easy to work with leather, if you know what your desired goal is. Leather has certain properties that make it perfect for beading.

• First of all, decide before you begin which is to be the right side of your leather, and which is to be the wrong side. Usually the glossy side is considered the right side. If you're working with suede or ultra-suede, it really makes no difference, except once you've decided that one side is your right side, you need to keep it that way.

• The needle should always pass through the leather in one direction. Leather has a tendency to curl, so if the needle goes into the WRONG side of the leather, and out the RIGHT side of the leather, your seedbeads will hug your cabochon and look better.

• For most beadwork, soft leather is easier to work with. Certain projects (cabochon earrings, etc.) which require fine stitching require softer leather. However, other projects (the moccasins) require stiffer leather. Boot leather can be used, but it is very thick and will break many needles. Make sure you have the proper needles for this. If you find you're having a problem with getting the needle to pass easily through the leather, you can pre-punch the leather on a sewing machine. Simply loosten the wheel and manually work the needle up and down to make the holes in your leather. Then, when you're ready to do your beadwork, the needle passes easily through your pre-punched holes.

• Leather has layers; when you are making a "Stay-Stitch" (stitching in place to give strength), you penetrate only the top layer, being careful not to go all the way through the leather.

• A "Whip-Stitch" is on the edge of the leather, traveling over the side. Your needle always moves in a circular motion as you work.

• Never make your thread so long that it tangles easily. The rule of thumb is the length of thread should be no longer than your arm can reach in one motion. For most people, this is 2-3 feet.

Ultra-suede can be substituted for leather.

• If you find you are allergic to nickel in jewelry, you may have a problem working with leather. Many of the compounds used to process leather create the same reaction as a nickel allergy would. Also, wearing leather jewelry can create an allergic reaction. If you find you're wearing only good jewelry and still have problems, switch from leather to ultra-suede.

Leather can be used in strips, pieces, and thongs. You can make a necklace on leather, you can tie strips onto necklaces, you can bead it, you can braid it.

Braiding leather is easy when both ends are open. It's a little harder when both ends are sealed. Remember in the '70's when we all tooled our own leather handbags? Remember how we braided the straps? (perhaps that was in another life). This is how to braid leather:

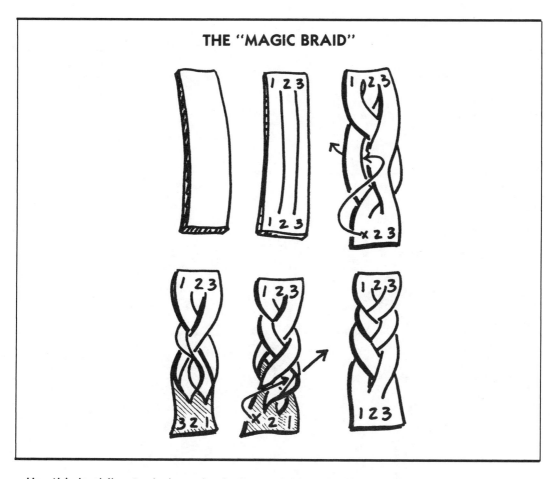

THE "MAGIC BRAID"

Use this braiding technique for belts, watchbands, hat bands, purses, etc.

Pi / Leather Necklace

One of the latest fashion trends is the "Pi Necklace". Using a Pi (ring-shaped) bead, it combines leather, Chinese coins, and surprisingly few elements to create a terrific necklace.

You need:

- 1 yard leather cord
- 2 Chinese coins
- 1 large Pi bead (2" in diameter)
- 3 small Pi beads

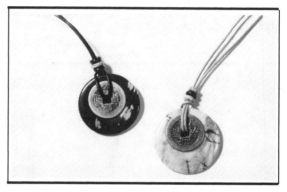

Step One:

Position the Chinese coins, one on each side of the Pi bead. Fold the leather cord in half, and thread the loop through the hole in the Pi.

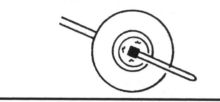

Step Two:

Secure with a Half-Hitch knot.

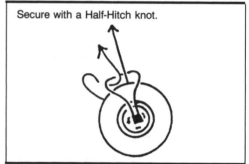

Step Three:

Thread on your three small Pi beads.

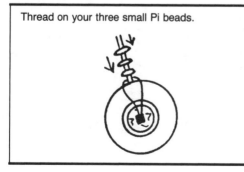

Step Four:

Secure the back with a leather clasp, a Slip Knot or an Overhand Knot. (Please see section on KNOTWORK).

Leather Stamping

If you like to work with leather, then you can stamp your own findings for a very unusual look. The stiff "saddle-bag" leather is perfect for stamping. Make your own custom earring findings, separator bars, even clasps out of leather.

You need to invest in a few good stamps, a mallet, and some good quality leather. To stamp the leather, you wet it, then emboss it with a hammer-and-chisel action of your mallet and stamp. You can then tan it, paint it, or bead it for a truly sensational look.

Some great stamps to use are:

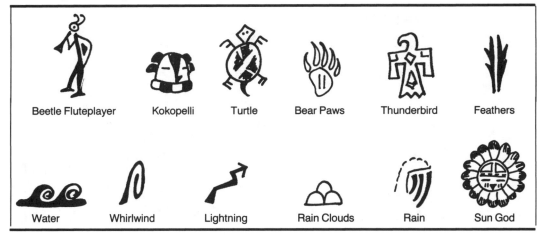

Beetle Fluteplayer   Kokopelli   Turtle   Bear Paws   Thunderbird   Feathers

Water   Whirlwind   Lightning   Rain Clouds   Rain   Sun God

Beaded Moccasins

We're not just talking about buying a pair and beading them, we're talking about making the moccasin from scratch, then beading it!

Supplies Needed:
- Two pieces of medium to stiff leather or suede, appx. 1 foot by 1½ feet (this differs based on foot size)
- Two pieces of muslin fabric the same size as above.
- One permanent marking pen
- Seedbeads
- Nymo thread in "F" weight
- Sharps #7 needle
- 1½ yards leather or suede thong
- Scissors

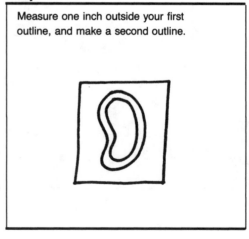

MAKING YOUR PATTERN:
Step One:

Outline the shape of your foot on each piece of muslin.

Step Two:

Measure one inch outside your first outline, and make a second outline.

Step Three:

Measure the distance from toe to heel. Make a mark at the halfway point.

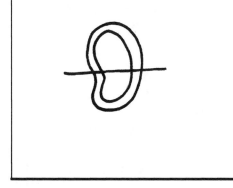

Step Four:

Measure out 3" beyond the outline in the back half only (this will become the back of the moccasin and collar). Think of this as piece "A".

Step Five:

Now, make a pattern for the top of the moccasin ("B"). Using the pattern from Step Three, and only ½ the length of the foot (front half). Round the end to make a "tongue" for the top of the moccasin.

Step Six:

Using the patterns you just made in the muslin, cut the pieces out in leather. Make sure you keep the right foot components separate from the left foot components, as your feet differ slightly.

ASSEMBLING YOUR MOCCASIN

Step One:

To make this come together correctly, you need to make the stitches on piece "A" twice as long as the stitches on piece "B". This will create that "puckered" effect.

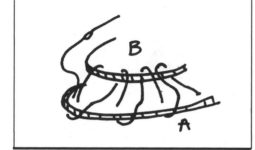

Step Two:

Center piece "B" over piece "A". You can pin this together at the center point, if it helps hold it in place. Starting at the instep, whipstitch on around with your THREAD DOUBLED for strength.

Step Three:

Cut notches in the back section of piece "A" (the heel). These should extend out evenly with the sides of the heel.

Step Four:

Stitch the notches closed. This give the back of the moccasin its "standing up" shape.

THE BEST LITTLE BEADING BOOK

Step Five:

Cut slits in the collar for the lacing material. This will act as a shoelace.

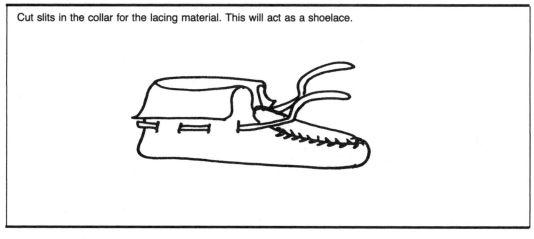

Step Six:

Now that the moccasin is constructed, it's time to embellish it. Stuff newspaper or paper towel into the toe so it keeps its shape as you stitch. Center your design. Using the tips in the BEADING ON FABRIC section, you can make a beautiful moccasin. When done, you can whipstitch with seedbeads over your seams.

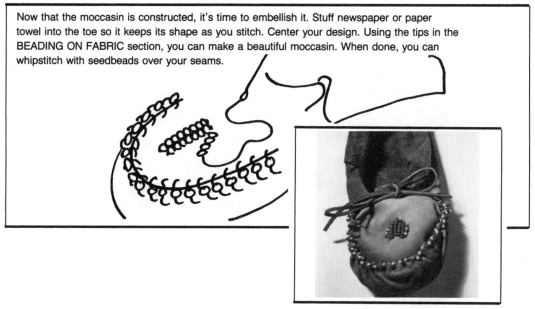

Knotted Cord Necklace

One of the newest looks is using a cording that shows with very few beads strung on. The beads are held in place with simple overhand knots. It's a very airy, pretty necklace, and you can use your heavier beads, because there are so few beads on this, it won't weight you down!

Supplies Needed:

- Three yards heavy thread (FFF weight silk or nylon, carpet or upholstery thread (conso), etc.)
- No more than twenty large to medium beads
- Cement

HOW TO DO IT:

Because your cord is stiffer than most, you don't need a needle. Put a little cement on the end to make a self-needle. Let it dry, then begin stringing. Make a square knot just before and after you have added each bead. Space them out by at least an inch or so, so that the cord shows. Make this long enough to go over your head without a clasp, and then complete as a continuous necklace.

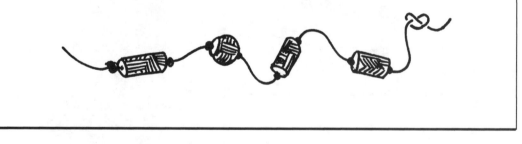

You can also try this with ½mm leather.

Trinket Tassel with Chinese Knotting

This easy, elegant necklace works up very quickly. Chinese Knotting is the newest update to the macrame knotting of the 70's. It takes a minimum of supplies, but with maximum impact!

Supplies Needed:

- 8 yards of satin "rat tail" cording (4 of gold and 4 of black)
- one large bead
- 24 gauge beading wire in black, 20 gauge in silver
- An assortment of beads, findings, charms, etc.
- A macrame board and "T" pins for holding down the knotwork
- Cement
- A chain nose plier

Step One:

Take a 4" length of your silver 20 gauge wire. Put the large bead on the center of this, then coil evenly on both ends, making sure that you have nice, large loops.

Step Two:

Using the black 24 gauge wire, start joining small segments of beads on wire, done in the same manner. This is to create a "fringe" effect. Remember, you want to keep the segments short, so that they have nice movement, and aren't stiff.

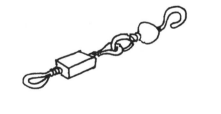

Step Three:

It's nice to add charms as you go. Three "fringes" are usually fine. It looks better if you stagger their length. You can either coil the wire, or bend it over to a neat loop (like the SIMPLE EARRING PROJECT).

Step Four:

Now that you're done with the fringe (bottom), you are ready to start knotting the rattail cord. Cut your rattail into 2-yard lengths Fold these in half. Attach them at the fold to the large ring at the top with a half-hitch knot.

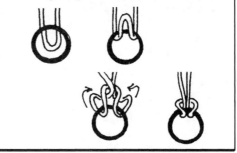

Step Five:

Make an overhand knot over your half hitch to secure.

Step Six:

It's easier to work on the knotting if you secure the beaded fringes and large bead by pinning or taping them down.

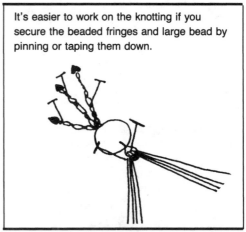

THE BEST LITTLE BEADING BOOK

Step Seven:

The secret to the beauty and simplicity of this piece is the variety of knotwork that can be done up the sides. You'll knot each side separately, but they should be matching. Please see the section on KNOTWORK for many choices of knots.

Step Eight:

Use your 20 gauge silver wire to make a hook-and-eye clasp at the ends. This eliminates the need for expensive findings. Make sure that you wrap your wire tightly, so the rattail doesn't slip out, then cement the rattail at the ends where your clasp is attached.

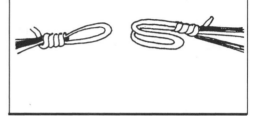

Another interesting variation is to use a Pi bead as your large bead, and attach by a half-hitch knot.

THE JOSEPHINE KNOT

Try using different dramatic color combinations in your rattail. No two necklaces ever look alike!

Knotwork Variations

Knotting is a fun and easy way to add elegance to your projects. Knots can be worked in leather, rattail, soutache, string . . . just about anything! Use these knots on the trinket tassel, for a closure on a garment; or work a decorative knot in a festive cord and lacquer it as a hair ornament or brooch.

There are thousands of knots . . . here are but a few. (Those of you with a Navy background — please forgive my use of the word "knot" when it's technically a "bend"!)

KNOTWORK

THE HALF KNOT

THE SQUARE KNOT
Also known as the REEF KNOT, it consists of two HALF KNOTS, worked right over left, then left over right.

THE BOX HITCH

THE GRANNY KNOT
A lot like the SQUARE KNOT, but it's worked right over right, OR left over left.

THE BEST LITTLE BEADING BOOK

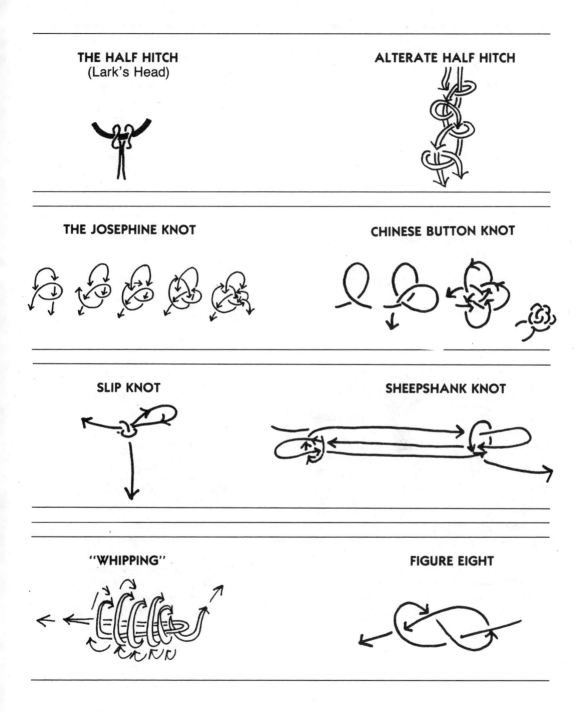

THE HALF HITCH
(Lark's Head)

ALTERATE HALF HITCH

THE JOSEPHINE KNOT

CHINESE BUTTON KNOT

SLIP KNOT

SHEEPSHANK KNOT

"WHIPPING"

FIGURE EIGHT

Working With Seedbeads

There are several stitches used when working with seedbeads. Due to their size, their usually worked in some kind of a weaving pattern. The stitch you use will govern the shape and overall effect of what you create, so it is important to be aware of the variations.

• **LOOM WEAVING** creates a perfectly squared off design (rank and file). It is perfect for adapting cross stitch patterns. The rows are build on a combination of thread and beads, created by interlocking the threads as they run through the beads.

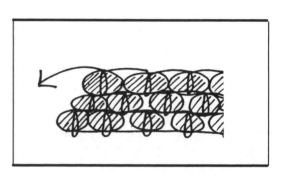

• **COMANCHE STITCH** creates a horizontal brink stitch. This is great for triangular effects. This is also known as the "Brick Stitch", the "Netting Stitch" and the "Peiute" stitch (not to be confused with Peyote). The difference between this and the other stitches is that the comanche stitch actually builds on the thread used. The beads are almost incidental to the construction. This stitch is created essentially by looping thread onto thread. You start with a base row and add on from there.

The beads in each row are offset because they need to catch the open area on the row below. Because this technique is usually worked with beads, the detailing of the stitches shouldn't show. Of course, as with all beadwork, you work as tightly as possible to create a nice, not-floppy effect. This stitch can be worked flat or circular, double-bead or single.

• **PEYOTE STITCH** creates a vertical brick stitch. The pattern is created by weaving through the beads. It can be worked flat, circular, or freeform, which involves adding larger beads and weaving them in in a random way. Very rarely can you do two freeform peyote projects and have them look the same! Beads can be worked doubled or single.

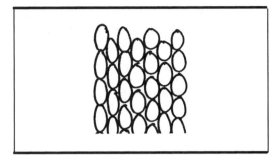

• **NETTED LACE** is an open weave that is more airy than the previous stitches. It can be worked both circular and flat.

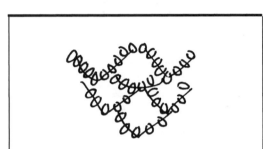

• **LACY PATTERNS:** There are many patterns that need to be explained in depth. Please see the following pages.

TIPS FOR WORKING WITH SEEDBEADS:

• If you purchased them on a hank, don't cut them off. It's much faster to transfer beads by connecting your needle to the existing thread and just sliding them across than it is to pick them up one by one.

• When you buy them, catalog the seedbeads for size so you'll know at a glance which size is which.

• Be careful of beads that are not colorfast or lightfast. Certain lined seedbeads will fade and lose their color; certain metallic beads loose their color just by being handled. If you've just spend 30 hours on a project, you don't want it fading!

• Check with your cleaner if you've beaded a project and you're getting it cleaned. They're notorious for cracking, melting, and ruining beadwork.

Fringing Techniques

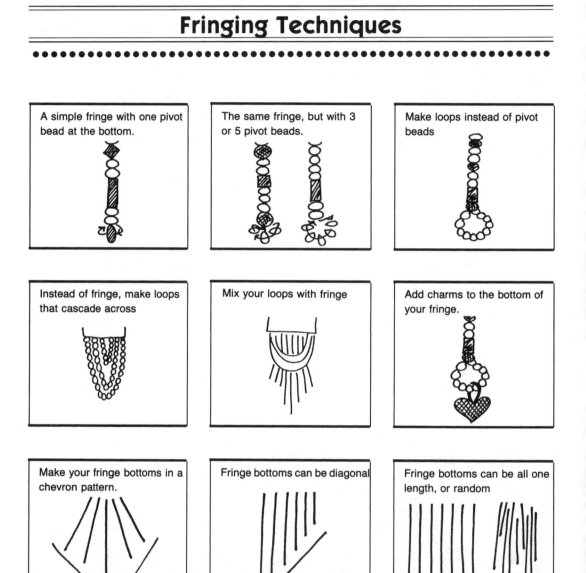

A simple fringe with one pivot bead at the bottom.

The same fringe, but with 3 or 5 pivot beads.

Make loops instead of pivot beads

Instead of fringe, make loops that cascade across

Mix your loops with fringe

Add charms to the bottom of your fringe.

Make your fringe bottoms in a chevron pattern.

Fringe bottoms can be diagonal

Fringe bottoms can be all one length, or random

You can plot out your fringe designs on graph paper.

THE BEST LITTLE BEADING BOOK

Comanche Stitch Earrings

These earrings are actually a combination of stitches, but the most recognized is the Comanche Stitch (also known as the "Brick Stitch") that makes the top part of the earring. These earrings are also known as "Triangle Top" and "Brick Stitch" earrings.

When you first look at these earrings, it may seem a little confusing as to where to start. What you need to do is mentally break them down into 4 parts.

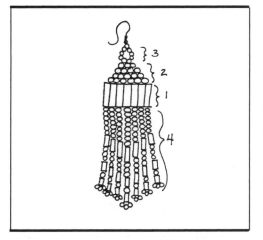

(1) is the base of the earring. You will start with this section. It can be composed of either bugle or seedbeads. This sets the tone for the earring: the number of beads here will eventually be your number of fringes when you are done.

(2) This is the actual Comanche Stitch. The number of beads will decrease with each row.

(3) This is the loop that attaches to the ear finding.

(4) This is your fringe.

Supplies Needed:

- Seedbeads of various colors to make a design.
- Bugle beads (any length will do, as long as they are all the same)
- Accent beads for your fringe (it's recommended that you keep them smaller than 4mm, to keep the earring light)
- Nymo in "0" or "00" weight
- English beading needle #10 or 12 (to fit your beads)
- Two earwires

Step One:

Cut 2 yards of nymo and thread your needle. You'll work single thread. Don't knot the end, leave a 2" tail that you can weave in later. Put two bugle beads on your needle.

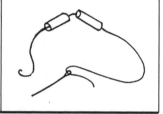

Step Two:

Bring the needle around and enter the same 2 beads again in the same order. As you pull tightly, they will fall into place "side by side", like 2 little sticks of dynamite.

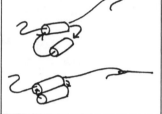

Step Three:

Reinforce by repeating this two more times. You'll add beads one at a time by repeating this stitch. Keep working until you have your earring the desired width.

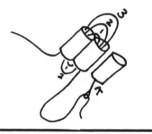

Step Four:

You just completed part (1). Now, on to part (2). This is the true Comanche Stitch. Turn your piece so that the thread is coming out of the right side top. If you are right handed, you will be working from right to left. Add a seedbead to your thread. With your needle, catch the little bundle of threads, and go back up thru the seedbead. It is very important that you go thru the bead in the opposite direction than you just did, or the bead will not lay right. The hole should be facing up. If it's facing sideways, you need to re-do that last step.

THE BEST LITTLE BEADING BOOK

Step Five:

Work across the row. When you get to the end, turn, and continue on across. Because your beadwork is actually building on the spaces between the beads, each row will have one fewer bead in it. Continue on until there are two beads in the row. You are now ready to start part (3).

Step Six:

This step is really easy: You're going to make the loop that holds the ear finding. Think of the last two beads in the top row as "A" and "B". Bring you needle out of "A", add 6 seedbeads, then go back down into "B". Repeat this a couple of times to strengthen the loop. This is where the earring usually breaks from wear and tear, so it's best to reinforce this. If your ear finding opens, you can add it in later. If it's the kind that doesn't open, you'll need to add it on after your third bead.

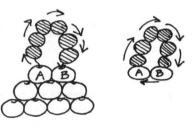

Step Seven:

You just completed part (3). Weave your thread down through the earring to the center bottom bugle. If you find you need to add new thread, simply weave in the ends from the first strand, anchor a second strand by weaving in the first end, then you're ready to continue stitching. Fringing is very easy. Start with the bottom center. Bring your thread out of the bottom of the center bugle. Add a few seedbeads, then an accent bead, more seedbeads, accents, etc. The bottom bead is your "pivot bead". You will go back up thru all of your beads except that one (if you go thru that bead, they will all fall off!). For certain designs it seems to work best to have your longest fringe in the center. As you work outward, shorten each fringe just a little. Work out in one direction, then back to center, and work out the other way. You can keep better track of your fringe by always working out from the center.

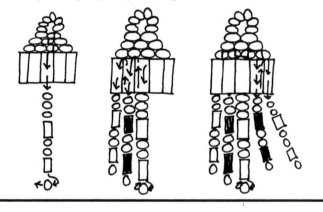

Step Eight:

Weave in all loose threads. If you haven't done so yet, add your earwire.

THE BEST LITTLE BEADING BOOK

Comanche Stitch Variations

WORK ON THE OUTSIDE OF A LOOP

Using a wire bead loop, add your Comanche Stitch to the outside, and dangle an ornament in the center.

WORK A CIRCULAR COMANCHE STITCH

It's almost as easy as the flat one.

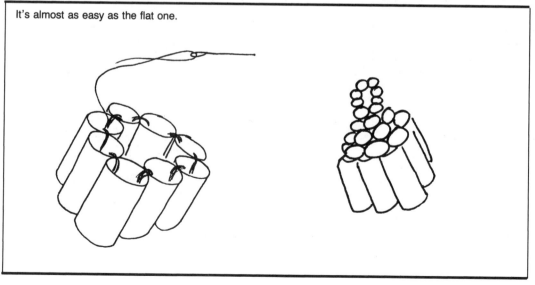

Huichol Earrings

The Huichol Indians of Mexico make many beautiful lacy designs in their beadwork. This is an adaptation.

It is recommended that you work with a 14° seedbead, because the larger beads just don't do this justice.

Always work in a circular motion (counter-clockwise) when you do this stitch.

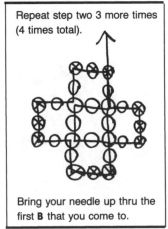

Supplies Needed:

- #12 or 15 English beading needle
- Size 14° seedbeads
- Nymo in "00" weight
- Cement
- Two earwires

Use four colors: **A, B, C,** and **D.** Work single thread. Start with a 3' length of nymo, and weave in new thread as needed. If you get one bead off it will mess up everything, so be careful your count is right.

Step One:

String on 8 of **A.** Bring thread thru all 8 beads again in a circular motion, then square knot your thread ends together.

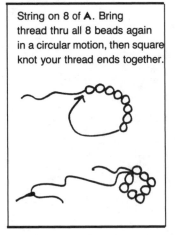

Step Two;

Add 1 of **A,** 3 of **B,** 1 of **A.** Skip the first **A** in the existing loop, then go thru the next.

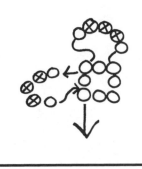

Step Three:

Repeat step two 3 more times (4 times total).

Bring your needle up thru the first **B** that you come to.

Step Four:

You'll be working your needle only thru the 1st and 3rd beads of **B** that you just added. Add 2 **B**, 1 **C**, 2 **B**, and bring the needle thru the 3rd **B** in what you just did. That's the pattern in this row: in and out of the 1st and 3rd **B**'s.

Step Five:

Go up thru the next **C** bead in line. Add 5 **C**, go thru the next **C**, add 5 **C**, thru the next **C**, etc. End by going thru **C** at peak (complete loop).

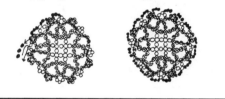

Step Six:

Bring needle thru the next 2 **C** beads. Add 3 **C**, skip 1 **C**, go thru 1 **C**, add 3 **A**, skip 3 **C**, go thru 1 **C**, add 3 **C**, skip 1 **C**, go thru 1 **C**, add 3 **A**, skip 3 **C**, go thru 1 **C**, etc. complete the row.

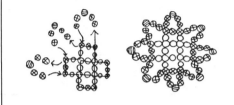

Bring your needle up to thru the bead at the "peak".

Step Seven:

Work "peak" to "peak" — Add 3 **D**, skip 3 beads, go thru 1**A** at "peak", add 3 **D**, skip 3 beads, go thru 1 **C** at peak, add 3 **D**, skip 3 beads, go thru 1**A** at peak, add 3 **D**, etc. Complete the row by going thru the last **C** at peak.

Step Eight:

Now we're not working counter clockwise, but back and forth. Go thru first **D**, then add 3 **B**, skip 1 **D**, go into next **D**, **A**, **D**, add 3 **B**, skip 1 **D**, go into next **D** and 1 **C**.

Step Nine;

Turn work, add 2 **B** and 2 **A**. Go thru **B** at peak.

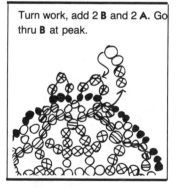

Step Ten:

Add 3 **B**, go thru next **B** at peak.

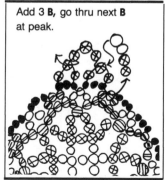

Step Eleven:

Add 2 **A** and 2 **B**, and bring loop down to **D**'s in previous row (3 **D**, 1 **A**, 3**D**) - backtrack

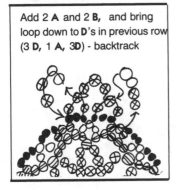

Step Twelve

Loop back up thru 1st 2 **B**, Add 5 **A**, skip next 4 beads, Go thru **B** at peak.

Step Thirteen:

Add 5 **A**, go back thru 2 **B**'s.

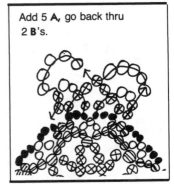

Step Fourteen

Loop thru **D**'s at base again, then up thru 2 **B** and 2 **A**.

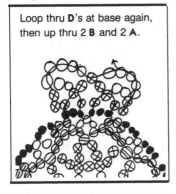

Step Fifteen:

Go thru 2 **A**, add 6 **B** (slip on earwire to fall halfway in this loop.

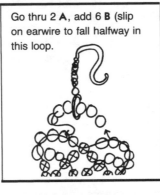

Step Sixteen:

Reinforce and weave in ends. WHEW! Work down to bottom to add loops. Use your existing rows of beads to anchor your loops. Cement & finish.

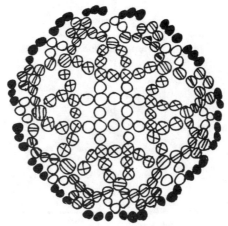

Peyote Stitches

CIRCULAR PEYOTE STITCH:

This is considered the easiest of the Peyote Stitches. Because it is worked in the round, it almost seems to "tell" you where the next bead needs to go.

Step One:

If you're beading around a cylindrical object (terminated crystal, pencil, etc.), fit the beads snugly around it, (make a little belt) and tie a square knot with the thread.
Go thru the first bead in your little "belt". *Drop down, add a new bead, and skip one bead.
Go into the next bead in your little belt. Repeat from the asterisk all the way around.

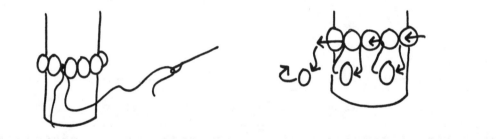

Your beads may flop around a bit at this stage, but don't worry — the next step will take care of that.

Step Two:

With this row, you'll "bridge the gap". You'll bring your needle alternately thru one existing bead in your beadwork, then add a new one where you have an empty spot. Continue around, then alternate the Step One with Step Two.

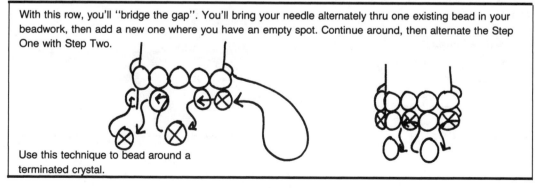

Use this technique to bead around a terminated crystal.

FLAT PEYOTE STITCH:

You'll work it with the same principle as above, but instead of working circular, you'll work it flat. You'll need to work-and-turn each row.

FREEFORM PEYOTE STITCH:

With Freeform Peyote, you add odd shaped beads, and work to weave them in. You will learn by practice how to fit the beads together in a neat way, and use the flat Peyote to fill in where needed.

Peyote Stitch Vegetables

You can make your own veggies using the Peyote Stitches.

Supplies Needed:

- #10 English beading needle
- Seedbeads
- Leather for cornhusks
- 4mm green beads for peas
- Nymo in 0 weight
- Cement

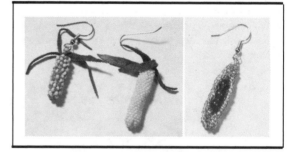

To Make Peas:

Start with 16 11° seedbeads. Work with the flat peyote stitch. Stitch your "peas" into the center, and partially weave your pod closed.

To Make Corn:

Use the same technique as for the peas, but completely close the cob. Work in yellow, or combinations of yellow and red ("Indian corn"). When done, stitch leather strips ("husks") to the top.

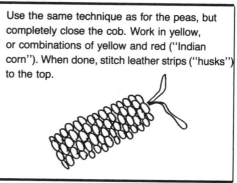

Also try carrots and red peppers using the same technique.

Making a Medicine Pouch

Several years ago, my mother and I went to hear a Curandera speak. The Curandera are considered faith healers in Mexico. This woman spoke of medicine pouches: that you make the pouch yourself, then you fill it with the things that matter most to you: your birthstone, your children's birthstones, a lucky feather, a coin, your baby's first tooth, etc. The meaning of this is that you focus your life on the most important things: as you fill your pouch, the Truth reveals itself to you: the true magic in life is what we make for ourselves. Creating and filling a medicine bag forces you to recognize which choices mean the most to you.

Making a medicine pouch with the peyote stitch is a lovely way to make your own magic.

Supplies Needed:

- #10 English beading needle
- Seedbeads
- A variety of accent beads
- Nymo in 0 weight
- Cement

Step One:

You will start out with a circle of seedbeads appx. 3" in circumference. You will work in two directions from this original circle. You will work downward, with both the Circular and Freeform Peyote Stitches.

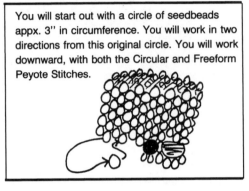

Step Two:

Continue working until you are at the point you wish to close up the bottom. You can weave your bottom ends to fit together.

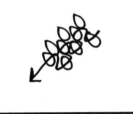

Step Three:

Using the Flat Peyote Stitch, weave upward to make a flap. You can decrease toward the end to make it taper.

Step Four:

Using the Flat Peyote Stitch, weave on a strap.

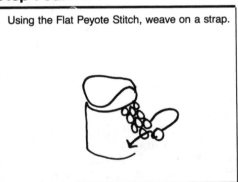

Pi Woven Necklace

This necklace starts out with larger beads, then you go back and embellish them with the Peyote Stitch (see back cover).

Almost any design will do, as long as you use Pi beads. The seedbeads and tile beads that you weave in and out of the Pi have a great look. Add Chinese coins, charms, and other fun embellishments, and cover as fully or as minimally with the Peyote Stitch as you like.

Supplies Needed:

- Two strands of 4mm black onyx beads
- One strand of 6mm black onyx beads
- One strand of 8mm black onyx beads
- Six Chinese coins with holes
- Two semi-precious Pi beads (1")
- One large semi-precious Pi bead (1½")
- One dZi bead
- Silk thread for stringing necklace
- Twisted wire needle for stringing necklace
- Nymo for embellishing with seedbeads
- #10 English beading needle for embellishing with seedbeads
- Cement

Step One:

String your necklace as shown. The ends should catch each other as shown.

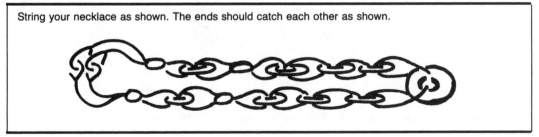

Step Two:

Embellish with the Freeform Peyote Stitch. Cover the Pi beads, the coins, etc. as fully as you wish. No two necklaces are ever alike.

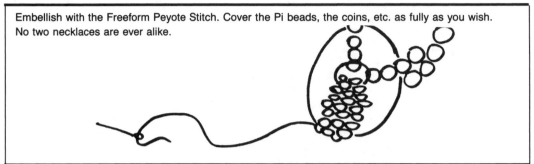

Beading A Bead

You can cover beads with seedbeads for unusual effects. Wooden beads with large holes work very well.

Method One:

Simply select a bead with a good-sized hole, and loop the seedbeads until it is covered.

Method Two:

Use the Circular Peyote Stitch to cover a bead. Start at one end and increase as needed.

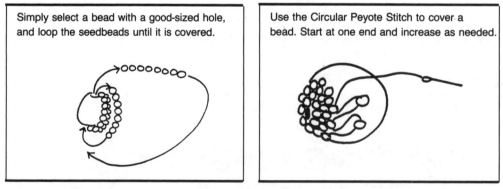

Use these techniques to also make beaded tassels. Simply add a fringe to the bottom of your bead.

Netted Lace Stitch

This can be worked both circular and flat.

Supplies Needed:

- Seedbeads
- Nymo in "0" weight
- #10 English beading needle
- Cement

Step One:

Make a horizontal row of 21 beads.

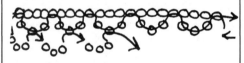

Step Two:

Work back to catch every 4th bead, adding 3 beads in the process. Work across the row. Second row: pick up the middle bead of the festoon you just added, and again, work skipping 3 beads, adding 3 beads, catching a bead, etc. Experiment with different numbers of beads and designs for different effects.

For the Circular Variation:

To make these earrings in my grandmother's design, work this netting stitch in a circular pattern.

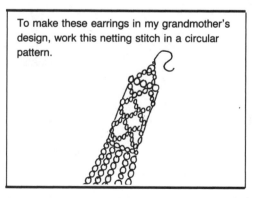

Circular Ring Earrings

Again, these start with that same lashing together that the Comanche Stitch utilizes, but you can use Chinese coins or semiprecious rings for many different effects.

Supplies Needed:
- #10 English beading needle
- Misc. seedbeads and crystal
- Two Chinese coins OR
  2 semiprecious rings
- Nymo in "B" weight
- Cement
- Two earwires

How To Do It:

Working the top part first: lash together 3 bugle beads as if you were making Comanche Stitch earrings. Out of the top of each one you will make a loop of 10 seedbeads, and catch the ring in this loop, then go back down into the same bugle bead you just came out of. When you have done this to all three, then on the opposite end of the bugle beads, Comanche stitch 2 seedbeads, and make a ring of 6 more for your earwires. Weave in, cement, and trim.

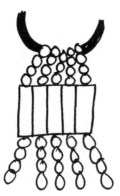

Make the same interlocking stitches with the bottom part, make your fringe, then cement and trim. Affix your earwires.

The Rainbow Earring

you'll start out the same as the Comanche Stitch, but the effect is very different.

Supplies Needed:

- #10 English beading needle
- 11° seedbeads in 6 colors
- Bugle beads
- Nymo in "B" weight
- Cement
- Two earwires

Step One:

Using two seedbeads of the same color, lash them together just as you would with the Comanche Stitch's first step. Plot out your colors (red, orange, yellow, green, blue, violet) with the reds on the outside. Your columns will run to a violet center, than back out in the opposite order.

Step Two:

Weave your way to the center, and add 5 violet beads to the violet column. Loop back down into the other violet column. Next, do the same thing by adding 10 blue beads. Make a little interlocking stitch to keep these two locked together. Now do the same by adding 17 green, then 19 yellow, 21 orange, and 32 red. As you stitch these rows to interlock, remember that the top six red beads need to be kept loose to affix the earwires.

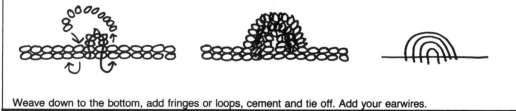

Weave down to the bottom, add fringes or loops, cement and tie off. Add your earwires.

On-Loom Weaving

You can buy or make your own bead looms. On-loom weaving has a very different look to it than off-loom — it's very structured.

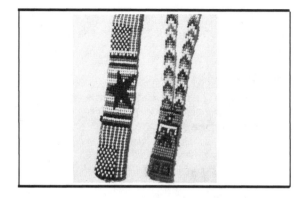

Supplies Needed:

- One bead loom
- Seedbeads
- Nymo in "0" weight
- #10 English beading needle
- Cement

Step One:

Thread your loom

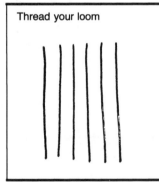

Step Two;

Weave a couple of rows of just thread in an over-under pattern to stabilize. Start on the right — tie this thread onto onto the right thread.

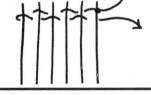

Step Three:

String on your beads. They will fill the gaps between the strands. You will have one less bead than the number of strands. Bring these beads underneath the existing threads.

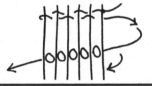

Step Four:

Bring the thread up over the top of the loom With your finger, push up the beads, and thread back thru them in the opposite direction. Be sure that the thread catches on the left strand, or they will all pull out.

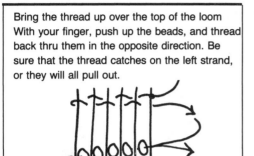

Step Five:

Add more beads, and repeat the process. Keep going until you have the right length. Weave a couple of rows of just thread (like you did at the beginning. Remove from loom. Fold over end threads and back with leather.

LOOMED NECKLACE ON COVER

To make the necklace on the front cover, you would start with 27 threads, that you cut extra long (You always need them longer than you think). Loom your centerpiece, then, divide design in half (for each side of necklace). Remove from loom and hand string each strand for about 4". Put each side back on loom, and loom smaller patterns individually (one for each side). The one shown is just a basic diamond pattern. When completed, remove again from loom and finish stringing up to back center. End as a multistrand necklace in multiple knot covers attached to the appropriate findings. Weave in your bottom strands by making a fringe. It's really a lot easier than it looks!

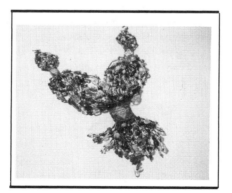

Basic Cabochon Earrings

These stunning earrings don't take long to make, yet their impact is amazing!

Supplies Needed:

- 2 cabochons (oval or round)
- Seedbeads (one or two kinds), 2-3 strands of each
- Nymo thread in "B" or "O" weight
- A small piece of leather (big enough for your 2 cabochons)
- 2 earring posts with backs (the kind with a flat front)
- 1 needle (sharps #7)
- Crafters' glue
- Embellishing beads (4mm or so) — glass, crystal, semiprecious for fringe
- Scotch tape

Step One:

Outline the shape of the cabochons on the WRONG side of the leather. Because cabochons differ in size, make sure that you you outline each one once, not the same one twice.

Step Two:

Carefully cut out each one, making sure that you cut evenly and don't leave any sharp edges to your outline. Follow the shape of the cabochon as closely as possible.

Step Three:

Roll a piece of tape with the sticky side out. Place on the wrong side of the leather, and lay the cabochon on the tape. This will temporarily hold the cab in place as you work.

THE BEST LITTLE BEADING BOOK

Step Four:

Thread a 3 foot length of thread on your needle. Working single thread, knot the end, and stay-stitch into the WRONG side of the leather Repeat this stitch in the same place, being careful not to go completely through the leather.

Step Five:

With your needle as close as possible to the edge of the leather, bring the needle thru the leather TO THE RIGHT SIDE. With your left* thumb facing the RIGHT side of the leather, you're ready to start stitching. You're now ready to WHIPSTITCH.

*If you're left handed, adjust according.

Step Six:

This sequence repeats from this point:

A. Add a bead

B. Working counter-clockwise, bring your needle through the leather to the left of the first hole.

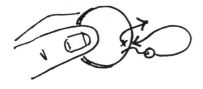

C. Bring your needle thru the bead you just added, from right to left (the direction you're working)

D. Keep repeating from "A" until you have completely filled the edge with beads all the way around.

Step Seven:

Pass your needle through the beads only (not leather) "drawstring"-style, and tighten to hug cab. Do a couple of staystitches in the wrong side of the leather to secure.
Now you're ready to start the fringe.
Remove the tape and the cabochon.

Step Eight:

Start with the bottom center. Your needle comes out of the right side of the leather. The longest fringe will be in the center. String several seedbeads. Add crystal, semiprecious, etc. The bottom bead is your pivot bead. Return back up thru the beads in this fringe.

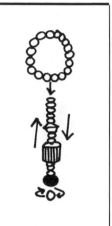

Step Nine:

Staystitch through the leather, and move over one bead width. Your next fringe will be modified to be slightly shorter. Keep working until you have the desired number of fringes.

For other fringing ideas, see the section on HOW TO MAKE FRINGES.

Step Ten:

Securely tie off your thread by staystitching on the wrong side. You're now ready to assemble the earring. Punch a small hole in the leather for the earposts (for pierced earrings).

Step Eleven:

Sandwich your components in this manner:

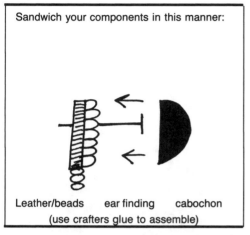

Leather/beads   ear finding   cabochon
(use crafters glue to assemble)

Step Twelve:

If making clip-on earrings, instead of piercing a hole in the leather, carefully cut a slit and slip in the clip-on finding. Assemble the same way.

By enclosing the finding, your earring has a more polished look.

A NICE VARIATION:

Glue a second cabochon on top of your completed earring.

You can also add charms in your fringe for a different look.

Fringed Seedbead Necklace

Even if you've never worked with seedbeads before, this is a fairly simple project. The foundation stitches are the same as the foundation stitches for Comanche Stitch earrings. It doesn't use many beads and it's very impressive when it's done, but it does require some time. The finished product is well-worth it!

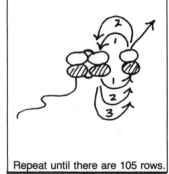

Supplies Needed:

- One hank of 11° seedbeads
- Nymo thread in "B" or "O" weight
- Two clamshell knot covers
- One clasp
- Cement
- #10 English beading needles
- #12 English beading needles (optional)
- A variety of accent beads (semiprecious and/or glass in 4-6mm)

Step One:

Cut 3 feet of nymo and thread your needle. You're working single thread. Thread on 4 seedbeads as shown.

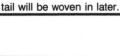

Leave a 2" tail at the end of the thread, with no knot. The tail will be woven in later.

Step Two:

In a circular motion, stitch the beads side by side. Repeat twice, working as tightly as possible.

Step Three:

Add new rows in groups of 2 seedbeads at a time in the same way. Reinforce as needed.

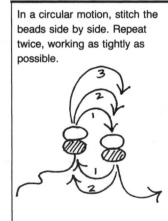

Repeat until there are 105 rows.

Step Four:

Now you're ready to start the fringe. I always work my fringe out from the center, so I don't lose track. Your center fringe is the longest (4½'') with the outer fringes being shorter. Each row of seedbeads has a fringe. Start your fringe with seedbeads, then add accent beads here and there. At the very bottom is the "pivot bead." Go back up through all of the beads, except for the pivot bead, and up through the original two beads. Travel over to the next row, and repeat, except this fringe is slightly shorter.

If you need to add nymo as you work, simply weave the end of the old thread in (trim), weave a few stitches with the new thread to secure, then continue on.

It's important to have an odd number of fringes, so that the center is the longest, and the focus point.

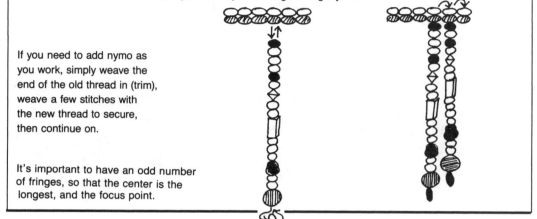

Step Five:

As you work outward, it's nicer if the corresponding fringes match (like a mirror image). You may need to switch to a #12 needle as you work if you find it's getting hard to get the needle through the beads. Be careful not to break a bead.

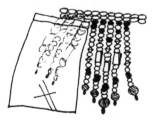

To keep the finished fringes out of your way as you work, put them into a little ziplock bag as you finish them.

Step Six:

Now that the fringe is done, you need a little row of reinforcing beads on the top edge (away from the fringe). These will appear to be laying on their sides.

Your thread will stitch under the little bundle of threads you created when you first lashed the rows together. You should add enough beads to completely fill in this row.

THE BEST LITTLE BEADING BOOK

Step Seven:

When you've completed the center section, it's time to add the part that will go around your neck. You need to measure how long you want this to be. Remember, it is a collar, so it shouldn't be too long. The one pictured here is 18'' including the clasp. If your center section is 4'' long, then you need another 14''. Divide that by 2, & each new part needs to be 7'' long. Cut new nymo 2' long, work double thread. Make a knot in the end, and place in knot cover. Add about 6½'' of seedbeads and accent beads, stitch through outside row of seedbeads, then adding more seedbeads, lock into place by passing through larger accent beads.

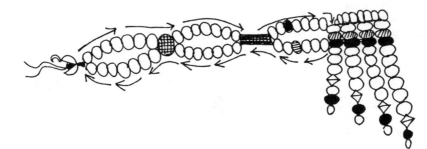

Return to knot cover,
make knot inside, and cement.
Repeat for second side.
Close knot covers and attach to clasp.

Peyote Stitch Around a Cabochon

This is actually a combination of Peyote Stitch and Netted Lace. It's a great way to bead a bezel for a really different look.

Supplies Needed:

- One large cabochon
- Seedbeads
- #10 English beading needle
- Nymo in B weight
- Cement

Step One:

String enough seedbeads to outline your cabochon. Work one row of Circular Peyote Stitch in each direction.

Step Two:

*Add 5, skip 3 beads in existing row, go into 4th bead; repeat from * all the way around (this is the Netted Lace Stitch). Tighten by filling in with 2 or 3 beads between the "peaks" of the last row (like a drawstring). Work tightly to encase the cabochon firmly. Add a loop on top to add a necklace or chain.

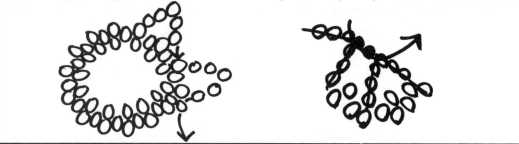

The Peyote Stitch Spoon

My friend, Alma, is Native American. She told me of a wonderful custom. When a baby is born, a spoon is given as a present. What sets this apart is the fact that the handle of the spoon has been beaded in the Peyote Stitch. Leather tassels hang from the ends. What a beautiful way to take your first meals!

The challenge is increasing and decreasing stitches to fit the spoon snugly. A baby spoon-in-the-making is on the back cover.

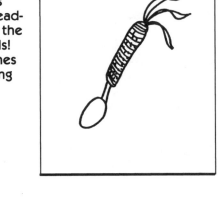

Supplies Needed:
- One sterling spoon
- #10 or #12 English beading needles
- Nymo in "0" weight
- A variety of seedbeads
- Leather strips
- Cement

HOW TO DO IT:

Working in a circular peyote stitch, start at the base of the spoon, about 1½" from the bowl end. Stitch up as far as you like. If you decide to cover the whole spoon handle, end by cutting the leather into fringes and sewing them on at the tip.

Totally Fringed Earrings

This is the design that my grandmother made for the Ziegfeld Follies. It's very easy to put together.

Supplies Needed:

- #10 English beading needle
- Black 3-cut seedbeads
- A variety of red crystal
- Nymo in "B" weight
- Cement
- Two earwires

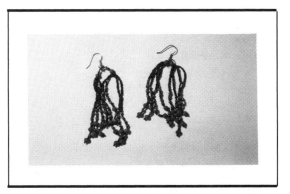

HOW TO DO IT:

String on one inch of black seedbeads, then one red crystal, a few more seedbeads, another crystal, etc. You'll make eight fringe per earring. Anchor this by stitching through 2 red beads. Your earwires attach at the top.

Dream Catcher Earrings

This very simple earring is very popular.

Supplies Needed:

- #10 English beading needle
- Nymo in "B" weight
- one turquoise chip
- Earring hoops
- Cement
- Two earwires
- A silver feather

HOW TO DO IT:

Starting at the top, attach your nymo and start weaving around the hoop. As you complete one round, loop the next row on the center of the previous loop. Keep working toward the center. String on the turquoise nugget and feather. Knot, cement, and trim extra thread.

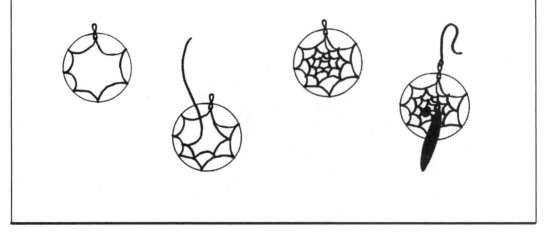

God's Eye Earrings

These were very popular in the seventies.

Supplies Needed:

- #18 gauge wire
- seedbeads
- #10 English beading needle
- Nymo in "B" weight
- Cement
- Two earwires

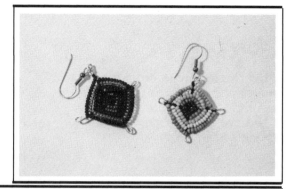

HOW TO DO IT:

Take your wire and bend it perpendicular into a cross. Foldover the ends to make loops. Starting at the center, string seedbeads on and loop around the wire. When done, cement, knot and trim your ends.

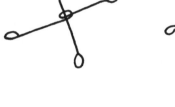  

LOOPY EARRINGS

Use the technique from the multistrand necklaces to make earrings.

Use eye pins and end cones and create some new looks.

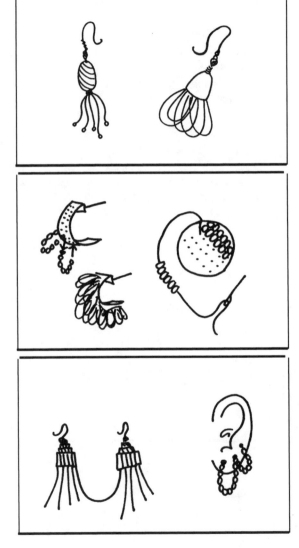

PERFORATED DISKS AND RINGS

Stitch into the perforated findings to try something new. If they have a squared pattern of holes, you can even do a mini "beadle-point" (bead + needlepoint) picture.

EARRINGS WIRED "IN SERIES"

If you know someone who has multiple pierced ears, it might be fun to make two pairs of earrings that share the outside fringe.

THE BEST LITTLE BEADING BOOK

Working With Polymer Clay

There should be warning label on this stuff that it's addictive! I cannot sit down to work with it without wanting to spend 12 hours! The results are fun and differsified . . . you can make some really interesting varieties of beads, findings, embellishments, and more.

Supplies Needed:

- As many colors of clay that you can afford (the more the better).
- A sharp matte knife.
- Wax paper or a smooth plastic placemat to work on
- Tape to hold your work surface down
- Cookie cutters
- Wooden skewer and/or hat pin to make holes
- Rolling pin
- Eye shadow
- Wire cheese cutter or clay cutter
- Your kid's clay tools

PREPARE YOUR CLAY BEFORE YOU BEGIN:

You must condition the clay before you can start. Roll it in your hands and manipulate it to soften it and make it easier to work with. You'll know the clay is ready when you can bend it and it doesn't break. A great way to make your job of conditioning easier is to tuck the clay (in a plastic bag) in a nice warm part of your body (huh?!). Your armpit, waistband, bra, or just sit on it! your body heat helps a lot in getting the clay soft enough to work with.

Sometimes the clay is hard (certain pigments are harder to work). A LITTLE vegetable oil can help (too much will bleed the color).

Step One:

The basic shape that you will use for just about everything is called a ROD (It looks like a snake). Roll it out. From this you can build many designs. Roll out a second rod. flatten it with your rolling pin, and encase the first rod with it (now it looks like one of those doggy snacks). This is a CANE.

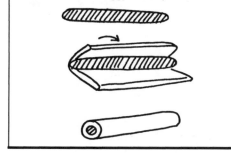

Step Two:

Keep wrapping layers on the cane, adding to the design. If you want stripes, layer the clay and slice, then apply as shown.

Roll the cane whenever you
need to smooth out the design.

Step Three:

Cut slices off of the cane and apply them to the sides of little balls of clay. The design will vary depending on the number used. This technique is called MILLEFIORI ("THOUSAND FLOWERS"). You can also wind extra clay between these to add a new design element.

Roll these in the palms of your hands to smooth out the design.

Step Four:

Use cookie cutters to make unusual designs. Stack the shapes that you cut out, and fill in the "negative space" with a different color. You can roll your canes smaller, and bundle them together for unusual effects.

As you work, try other shapes besides round beads.

Step Five:

MAKING FACES: There are many ways to do this, but this is my way: Think of scan lines on a TV. Starting at the chin, work your way up. Add a mouth, cupid's bow, nose, nostrils, bridge of nose, 2 eyes, forehead, widow's peak, and hair. Add clothes, earrings, etc. You can be as detailed with this as you like. Remember: you're making a cane, so make sure it's long (in the beginning it will look like a hot dog in a bun).

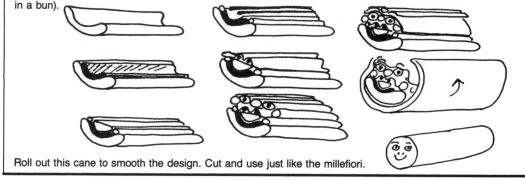

Roll out this cane to smooth the design. Cut and use just like the millefiori.

Step Six:

Try using a clay extruder (like a garlic press) to make different shape little rods that you can mix (squares make a great checkerboard).

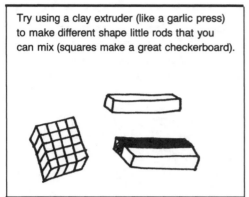

Step Seven:

Use leather stamps to emboss fancy designs.

There's always just plain freeform molding, too.

TO BAKE:

Follow package directions — be careful NOT TO BURN this — it's not good to smell! Lay your clay on the matte side of aluminum foil, hole side down. I use a toaster oven, so I don't recommend suspending the clay, because it puts it too close to the heating element.

Before you bake, you can brush lightly with eye shadow to give it a metallic sparkle.

AFTER you've baked it, you can glaze it to be shiny (the glaze could catch fire if you try to glaze it before you bake it).

ONE LAST NOTE:

Once you've used your utensils for this clay, you should not use them on food again.

Enhancing Wooden Beads

It's very easy to make your own designs on wooden beads. You can go as crazy with it as you like, or make something elegant and subdued!

Supplies Needed:
- Wooden beads
- PERMANENT marking pens in assorted colors
- Various acrylic paints
- White vinegar
- Spray fixative

Step One:

Clean your wooden beads in white vinegar before you start. Let them dry completely.

Step Two:

Plan your designs in pencil first.

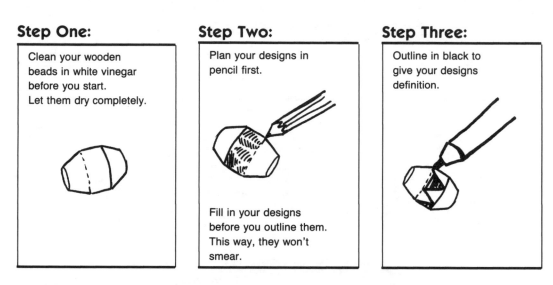

Fill in your designs before you outline them. This way, they won't smear.

Step Three:

Outline in black to give your designs definition.

Step Four:

Let them dry completely. Do not handle them a lot until you have "fixed" them, or the color could smear. When completely dry, spray lightly with the fixative.

Another fun thing to do is to airbrush your wooden beads. You can buy an inexpensive airbrush at an art supply shop.

Airbrushes use a stream of air that shoots the paint in a nice, delicate manner on the surface you're painting.

Other Handmade Beads

HANDMADE GLASS BEADS

Using a hand-held torch, you can work with glass to make incredible hand-made beads. The process requires special tools, but the results are quite beautiful.

GLASS BEADS IN YOUR MICROWAVE

You can purchase a special kiln for your microwave that boosts the temperature inside to get hot enough to fuse glass. The results are quite amazing (see page 71), and it doesn't hurt your microwave.

PLASTIC STRIPS

Strips made of meltable plastic can be molded into unusual beads, ornaments and embellishments. Once molded, you can affix rhinestones, beads, and sequins to enhance. There are two ways to heat the plastic to melt.

IN THE OVEN: Bake at about 225° for one minute (this will vary with your oven and brand of plastic). Lay on cookie sheet to bake. Remove from oven when adequately melted. While still warm, you can manipulate.

IN WATER: Put one inch of water in an electric skillet, and allow to almost start boiling. Submerge a section of plastic strip for 10 seconds (this will vary depending on your skillet, the pigment in the strip, and other factors). You can manipulate the strip while it is still in the water with a popsicle stick (if it sticks, use vegetable oil on the stick first). Remove from water and work quickly to shape. Plastic cools fast, and this limits your manipulating time.

PAPER BEADS

You can make beads out of old magazines, wallpaper, contact paper, old greeting cards,or your stationery if you like! All you need to do is cut long triangles out of paper, and roll them up. Contact paper and wallpaper are the easiest, because they are self-adhesive. You can use white glue to secure the other papers. Roll them on a toothpick or skewer (to allow for the hole), and let dry overnight.

Hat Pins

This season's quickest and most popular accessory is the hat pin. Make it elegant, with crystals and pearls, or make it earthy with semi-precious beads.

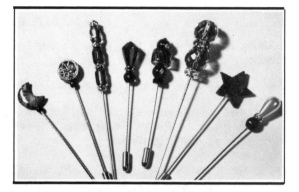

Supplies Needed:
- Hat pins
- "527" brand cement
- Variety of beads, charms, etc.
- Rhinestones (optional)

METHOD 1: USING A STRAIGHT HATPIN
Step One:

Design your pin by positioning the beads on the pin shaft

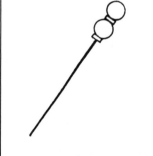

Step Two:

Pull the beads down and coat the shaft with cement.

Pull the beads up into position on the pin shaft, and allow to dry.

Step Three:

For a more polished look, you can place a small rhinestone into the hole at the top of the bead.

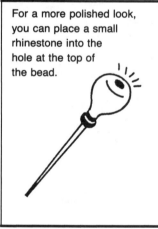

METHOD TWO: USING A HATPIN WITH FLAT PLATFORM

Lay out your design on the little platform, remove beads, apply cement, reapply beads, and let dry.

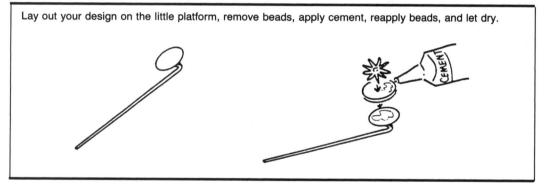

Alternative Assembling Techniques

You can make jewelry with almost any adhesive. The most important factor to consider when choosing an adhesive, is what will it do to your jewelry? (Please see page 38.)

CEMENTING STONES ON SUNGLASSES:
Apply the cement (E6000) to the sunglasses, then drop the stones on the wet cement. They will catch. You may need to do this several times to get the fullness.

STONE COVERED BRACELET:
Using the same method as above, cover the cuff bracelet in stones. Line the inside with ultrasuede.

PAPERCLIP BROOCH:
Dribble a mound of 527 on wax paper. Drop a handful of paperclips on the wet cement. When dry, use 527 to attach the brooch backing.

JAZZY EARRINGS:
Use a hot glue gun to make beautiful earrings with rhinestones.

NUTS AND BOLTS BROOCH:
Cement old car parts for a really unique brooch (these are old hose clamps, screws, etc.)

There's no limit but your imagination!

Origami Earrings

These earrings are great fun and very easy to make. You can make them with old wrapping paper, fabric that you have stiffened with fabric stiffener, aluminum foil, contact paper, wall paper, gum wrappers . . . anything that you can fold! It's recommended that you practice first on paper, then try experimenting with other media.

I must confess that my daughter, Joni, is the expert here . . . she folds them and I attach the earwires. Here's Joni's instructions:

Supplies Needed:
- Two pieces of paper, 6" square
- Two earwires
- Two jumprings
- Two fishing swivels

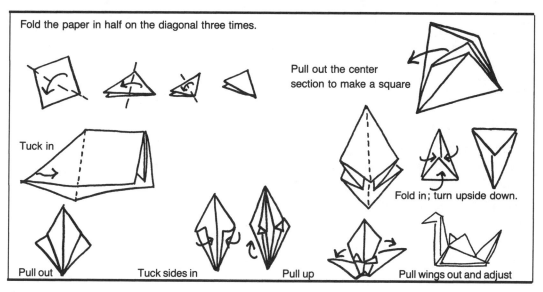

Fold the paper in half on the diagonal three times.

Pull out the center section to make a square

Tuck in

Fold in; turn upside down.

Pull out

Tuck sides in

Pull up

Pull wings out and adjust

When you're done folding, use a hole-punch to make the hole on the crane's back, then add the swivel and earwire.

Jewelry Styles Through The Years

When you're putting your jewelry together, it helps to have a style in mind.

• **PRIMITIVE JEWELRY** is characterized by the rough, natural, earthy shape of the components. It looks like it would be in a museum with an exhibit of old artifacts. Colors are usually subdued, deep browns, greens, and charchol.

• **THE EGYPTIAN LOOK** is usually done in brushed gold and deep navy blue. The shapes are somewhat geometric and flat; simple and elegant.

ROCOCO is recognized by its opulent, elaborate patterns, and lots of gold filigree. It's a "let them eat cake" attitude of conspicuous consumption. Rich gold and jewel tones abound.

CLASSIC looks never go out of style. The clean lines and good taste never go out of fashion. Creams and taupes are the usual.

VICTORIAN JEWELRY has a heavy and ornate look. Marcasite, black onyx, jet, and enamel have a somber quality. Also seen in a lighter form with pearls and hearts.

ART NOUVEAU has a beautiful, well-designed quality. You'll see echoes of nature in swirling shapes.

ART DECO has strong, very geometric lines obsessed with technology and speed. You'll see lots of arrows and greyhounds; elaborate designs set in marcasite, a juxtaposition of textures and materials make this very interesting.

THE CUBIST LOOK has clean, strongly geometric lines, with strong primary colors.

ATOMIC AGE jewelry is what most of us grew up with — you know the look ("Hollywood sunglasses and poodle skirts") — rhinestone sweater clips. Fifties rhinestone jewelry is making a comeback — incorporate it with your beadwork.

THE SIXTIES look is back again — tie-dye and large ceramic beads.

THE BEST LITTLE BEADING BOOK

Creating a Dramatic Portfolio

One of the most important keys to selling your jewelry successfully is in the presentation of your jewelry. Nowadays, it's not just enough to be a talented jewelry designer . . . you must also be salesman, photographer, and businessman.

There are many ways to present your jewelry.

1. **Make duplicates of your jewelry.**
   Don't just make one of an item . . . it's best to make two. One to sell (at a moment's notice), and one for a sample in your sample case. You'd be amazed at how quickly these disappear, and then you're left with nothing to show prospective buyers.

2. **Make photocopies of your jewelry.**
   It's best to make color photocopies of your jewelry. This way, should you need to reference them (and no samples are available) you remember which was which. Many times, someone will call you and say, "Remember the necklace you made for Mary Smith? I want one just like it." If you have a record, you'll know exactly which piece it was and what it cost.

   It's also recommended that you keep one copy for yourself (this could even be black and white photocopies) with your actual cost for each bead listed. Then, should you need to duplicate it, you'll know what it cost you last time to make it, and what it costs this time. If the cost of your materials have gone up, then you may need to adjust your prices. Always keep a record of the selling price and date, too.

   Keep a notebook of color photocopies to take to customers. This can act like a portfolio. This is a lot easier than carrying tons of your stuff.

3. **Make an attractive presentation of your jewelry.**
   Don't just assume that tossing your jewelry into an old cigar box will increase sales. IT WON'T! An off-beat, funky presentation will hurt your sales. An attractive, polished presentation means a professional portfolio, a briefcase, or a sample case made specifically for jewelry.

   Make attractive earring cards and necklace tags. You can use your business card, or have matching ones printed when you print your cards.

   If you don't want to have them printed, you can make your own using felt pens and thicker paper (known as cardstock). You can watercolor and paint on these, then write your company name in a metallic marker to give it a very boutique-look.

   In your sample case, you always want to have business cards and invoice books, so you can be prepared to write an order on the spot. Don't always assume your memory will hold for what they ordered. It's best to write items, prices, etc. down on an order form, and be able to give the customer a copy. Professionalism makes points. Your customers will know they can rely on you not to be "flaky".

THE BEST LITTLE BEADING BOOK

239

4. **Should you photograph your jewelry?**

   Actually, good photographs are a very professional thing to leave with key buyers.

   To photography professionally, you need: a good 35 mm camera with closeup lenses and automatic/manual focus; a tripod; a well-lighted area (with very balanced lighting). Place two lights at 45 degree angles to the camera. Your main light is your key light, the second one is necessary as a fill light, to fill in shadows. You really don't want to use a flash, because it gives that "mug-shot" look. If you don't have proper lamps, make sure your available light is good.

   When you compose your shots, make sure that the background is clean and uncluttered. Our eyes tend to ignore the background, but the camera is very literal, and EVERYTHING will be in your pictures. It's best to use a midtone gray background, so that your light meter will register more accurately. Also, it will give uniformity to your pictures, and the colors in your photos will be closer to the actual jewelry.

   To shoot slides, you need to purchase EKTACHROME or FUGICHROME film. Any film that ends in "Chrome" is a slide film. 100 ISO is a good speed when your light is adequate. 400 ISO is good for low-light situations.

   To shoot color prints, you need EKTACOLOR, KODACOLOR, or FUGICOLOR. Any film that ends in "Color" is a color print film. The same ISO numbers as listed above will work.

   To shoot black and white prints, you need special black and white film. Some films are better for contrast, although good lenses will compensate for most problems. Plus-X or Tri-X are fine.

   You may need to compensate for color changes due to your lighting: household lamps (tungsten lamps) make things red; fluorescent lights turn things green. You can purchase film that color-corrects this, or corrective lenses do the trick. Blue lenses correct tungsten, magenta corrects fluorescent.

5. **Whenever possible, include actual samples of your work in your portfolio.**

   Twenty GOOD samples are a good selling tool. Less than that is iffy, more than that, overwhelming. If you're not proud of the piece, DON'T include it . . . you should never have to make apologies for your work.

6. **Invest in good glass-top boxes.**

   These make a very nice presentation.

7. **Don't just have a handful of loose photos . . . mount them!**

   Use museum board to make a nice presentation. Use a spray adhesive so your photos aren't all lumpy and bumpy on the board.

8. **When selling your jewelry, make an appointment before you go see the buyer.**

   Don't just show up with your stuff. Nothing is as thoughtless as not calling ahead, and dragging in 3 boxes of jewelry, and demanding an audience! Get the buyer's name, and make a definite appointment. And, for heaven's sake, don't bug the person. There's a difference between making an impression and making a dent! Let the beauty of your jewelry speak for itself.

Starting a Home-Based (Jewelry) Business

This section is meant as a guide only, and in no way takes the place of sound legal advice. When starting a business, it is sometimes recommended that an attorney's services be utilized.

If you're going to start a business from your home, it is a good idea to first check local zoning laws. Certain condos or planned communities with CC & R restrict the types of activities that can be done from a residence. Once that is done, the next steps are:

1. Get a permanent mailing address.

If your business is jewelry-related, it might be safer not to operate with your home as your mailing address. Many government agencies (local and otherwise) are now allowed to sell your information. If your home address is linked to the fact that you're making jewelry, it could be unsafe. Mail box drop offices work well or post office boxes might be a good solution.

2. File a fictitious name statement.

A fictitious name statement protects your good name. It means that no one else in your county can take your business name. It is highly recommended that you get this filed. This may change from county to county, but for the most part, fictitious names statements are good for five years.

You'll go to your County Registrar's office and look in the files to make sure that no one already has the name you've chosen. Once you know it is clear, then you can file the name for yourself. If the name is taken, then you must pick out an alternative. You'll pay a fee (usually less than $20) to file the paperwork. Within 30 days, you must post it in a local newspaper. It must run for 4 consecutive weeks as a public notice, then be cleared again with the Registrar's office. If you fail to do this within 30 days, you might lose the right to the name.

Most local newspapers these services, which do include the final clearing.

3. Obtain a State Resale Number.

Through the State Board of Equalization, you can obtain a resale number. This means that when you purchase the SUPPLIES FOR YOUR BUSINESS (NOT PERSONAL GOODS), you don't pay sales tax. You will then charge sales tax to your customers. The good things about having a resale number include that you will then have access to new vendors who only sell wholesale (and you won't have to pay sales tax on the items you're reselling). The more serious thoughts to consider are that you MUST keep accurate records of your sales. You'll file returns on a timed basis (quarterly, monthly, annually, bi-annually). Your books are open to inspection by the state. If you are less than honest in your figures, you could risk an audit. Good record keeping skills are manditory. (You can buy a book on how to do bookkeeping for a small business at a bookstore). In many states, there is no charge for the resale number. This is good for as long as your business is operating.

4. Get a business license.

If you have a resale number, you MUST have a business license (there are fines if you don't). Fees for this range from $15 to $150 per year, depending on the city you live in.

Certain communities will charge you based on your income. Be sure to check that at the time you sign up. The business license is renewed every year.

5. Now you're ready to print business cards.

Many printers offer special prices on cards (also try those big discount office supply places). Choose a paper other than white, so it stands out from the others. Interesting graphics, bright ink, and a nice design can only enhance your reputation as an artist. At the same time, you might think of printing earring cards and necklace tags. NEVER print your home address on the cards; if you don't have a p.o.box, then print the cards with your company name and phone number, and the words "By appointment only". Mom was right: never let strangers into your home. Arrange to meet them at a local restaurant if they want to see your jewelry. It is also recommended that you do not go to a stranger's home to show your jewelry.

6. Promoting yourself.

Word-of-mouth is by far the best way to promote your new endeavor. Wear your creations often. Many times people will buy them right off of you. Pass your business card around freely.

Craft shows are an excellent way to build a client base.

Close to Christmas time, take a nice PROFESSIONAL LOOKING display of your wares to office buildings or industrial parks. Do not bother anyone who has a No Soliciting Sign. If it's okay with the people who own those businesses, then perhaps you can make some sales to employees during break time.

7. Get a good book on how to operate a business.

One of the best investments you'll ever make is to buy a book on operating a small business. The information is so valuable, you'll be very glad you did!

GOOD LUCK! No one said it's going to be easy! But with the right attitude and your wonderful creations, you'll go far!!!

THE BEST LITTLE BEADING BOOK

Healing With Stones — The Chakras

Many people believe in the power of crystals and gemstones. Because of the differing frequencies of the vibrations that each give off, they are thought to correlate to different parts of the body, and/or areas of one's life. When you consider that crystal oscillates (vibrates) and that quartz crystal watches are powered by these vibrations, it does seem to make a lot of sense.

As for powers of healing, I can cite from my own experience: with my first child, I spent a gruelling 23 hours in labor. While looking for an easier way with my second, I learned that moonstone helps women giving birth. So, when I went into labor, before leaving for the hospital, I wrapped a moonstone necklace several times around my left wrist. (Left is the side the body absorbs with, right the side that flows outward). Call it placebo, call it what you will: I had a 2½ hour labor, with no medication of any kind! Of course, if you have a serious medical problem, you should consult a physician. But, if you want an extra bit of something working in your favor, it couldn't hurt to find a stone that correlates and try wearing it for awhile!

It's believed that there are seven regions of the body. These regions (called chakras) correlate to the colors of the spectrum. White light can be split to become a spectrum. The spectrum is believed to contain powers in each of its colors. The seven healing zones (or chakras) are governed by color and light, and there are certain gemstones and crystals connected to each.

1. First Chakra — The Root/Base of Spine . . . . **(Physical)**
Red is both an earth and fire color, and denotes the fire and passion of life (see color section). In its most basic form, it is blood, fire, and the color most associated with the life force. This is the Chakra associated with the blood, energy, and circulation.
HEALING STONES: Red Coral, Garnet, Red Jasper, Ruby.

2. Second Chakra — Sex and Internal Organs . . . . **(Physical)**
Orange is also both an earth and fire color. But whereas red is blind passion and energy, the orange is qualified by the presence of yellow, which gives focus and direction. This Chakra governs the internal organs.
HEALING STONES: The stones that work with it are the orange-hued stones: Carnelian, Orange Jasper, Fire Opal, and Moonstone.

3. Third Chakra — Solar Plexus & Nervous System . . . . **(Physical)**
Yellow is a fire color. It symbolizes the sun, and contains a great power. It is for this reason that it works on this chakra. Isadora Duncan, the great dancer, believed that the center of one's being lie in the solar plexus. Yellow stones add equilibrium to your life.
HEALING STONES: Amber, Citrine, and Yellow Topaz.

---

4. Fourth Chakra — The Heart . . . . (Physical)

The fourth chakra is governed by the color green. This makes perfect sense because green is the color of life and growth. Green is calm, steady (not wild and erratic) growth, symbolized by the steady beating of one's heart and the nourishing of the body from the blood pumped by the heart. Green is energy, health and well-being in a pure form.

HEALING STONES: Aventurine, Chrysoprase, Emerald, Jade, Green Jasper, Malachite, Peridot.

5. Fifth Chakra — Neck & Throat . . . . (Spiritual)

At this point, we enter a more spiritual plane. Blue governs this chakra, which brings eloquence in speech, purity, and calmness. Blue is the color of verbalizing one's thoughts (putting them into words) and of true love.

HEALING STONES: Aquamarine, Blue Topaz, Turquoise, Lapis Lazuli.

6. Sixth Chakra — The Brow . . . . (Spiritual)

Associated with indigo (a mix of blue and purple hues), it combines the best of both. This governs the brow (or as some believe, the "Third Eye"): wisdom, intelligence, and insight. This region is for healing mental distress, and gaining insights into one's life.

HEALING STONES: Sapphire, Azurite.

7. Seventh Chakra — The Crown . . . . (Spiritual)

The most spiritual of all, this is the highest plane one can operate on. The color of true faith, spiritualism, and things much larger than man himself. This is the plane for faith, sleep, and other highly spiritual states. Purple and violet are the colors.

HEALING STONES: Amethyst, Fluorite.

The chakras start at the base of your spine (your root), and move upward from there.

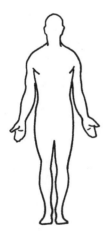

7. Seventh Chakra - Top of Head, or Crown	**VIOLET**
6. Sixth Chakra - The Brow, or "Third Eye"	**INDIGO**
5. Fifth Chakra - Neck & Throat	**BLUE**
4. Fourth Chakra - Heart	**GREEN**
3. Third Chakra - Solar Plexus	**YELLOW**
2. Second Chakra - Sex & Lower Internal Organs	**ORANGE**
1. First Chakra - Root (Base of Spine)	**RED**

Meanings of Stones

In addition to the Chakras and their correlating colors and stones, each stone is believed to have unique properties. Some of the following are old folk-beliefs, some cultural beliefs.

AGATE — Believed to be the 8th stone on the Breastplate of the High Priest. Closely correlated to the "Third Eye", it symbolizes man's inherent "love of good". Agate appears in a variety of colors, both opaque and translucent. Generally considered a lucky stone. **FIRE AGATE** helps diminish diabetes, and increases spiritualism; **GRAY AGATE** aleviates a stiff neck, and helps promote eloquence. Also has calming properties. Used to banish fear, and cool fevers. It's said to be able to cool boiling water; protection from snake bikes or poisons; and protection for children. Good for one's career; protects one from schemers; **GREEN AGATE** brings abundance, luck, wealth, longevity. Helps one to breathe better. Also said to be a fertility stone. There's an old folk-belief that if a woman is barren, she should drop a green agate into a glass of water and drink the water. (Supposedly) this makes her fertile. Also improves one's eyesight; **MOSS AGATE** brings a good harvest for farmers; **RED AGATE** (See Carnelian).

ALEXANDRITE — Good luck; heightens ability to experience joy.

AMBER — Purification. Helps with headache, jaundice, rheumatism, and toothache. Attracts compassion; protection from evil eye. A piece of amber placed on the forehead cools fevers; also enhances hearing.

AMETHYST — Believed to be the 9th stone of the Breastplate. A neck pendant made of amethyst controls the temperament. It's also said to dissolve blood clots, improve breathing, cure headaches and toothaches, promote clear thinking, and keep your mate faithful. If you place an amethyst under your pillow, it will bring you good dreams. Many other beliefs connect the amethyst to alcohol. If one never takes the stone off, it is said to give immunity to the effects of alcohol. If one is drunk, dropping the Amethyst into a glass of water and quickly drinking the water is said to make them sober (this is not recommended - one might swallow the stone). In the Middle Ages, Bishops wore the stone because they believed it promoted humility, sobriety, temperance, and wisdom (Amethysts are sometimes called "Bishop's Stone"). Brings inner peace and enlightenment, heals the "soul".

AQUAMARINE — Meditation, serenity, peace. Brings hope (a good stone to give to a depressed person). Lucky for sailors; a mystic stone with strong ties to the ocean.

AVENTURINE — Cures skin ailments; good luck for gamblers and lovers; enhances creativity.

AZURITE — Calming; brings peace against anguish. Introspective, good for meditation: its psychic properties are very powerful. Some call it "Lapis Linguis" and say it "sings".

BERYL — 10th Stone of Breastplate. Cures laziness; makes one inconquerable; gives insight and motivation; builds harmony. Cures sore throats and ailments of the jaw; **GREEN BERYL** helps eye infections; **YELLOW BERYL** is good for troubles of the liver. It also said to free one from bewitching spells.

BLOODSTONE — Heals organs, good for the blood (can help stop bleeding). Brings prosperity, balance; Gives strength to those who exercise; protection from adversaries' plans; helpful for confrontations; can bring on a tempest.

BONE — Cure backache, cramps, and toothaches.

BRASS — Diminishes suffering; represents immortality because it wears well against time.

BRONZE — Character strength, longevity, relaxation.

CARNELIAN — Helps your body absorb vitamins, minerals, and other nutrients. Also used as a protection from spiders and scorpions; can ward off the evil eye. If triangular-shaped, cures stomach and liver ailments and gum disease. Stops nosebleeds, protects from the evil eye. Enhances enjoyment of life, and gives courage and motivation.

CHALCEDONY — Helps with skin ailments; makes one more optimistic. Cures depression.

CHRYSOBERYL — Brings out goodness in people; promotes clear thinking.

CHRYSOCOLLA — Promotes inner peace, calms ulcers.

CHRYSOPHASE — Calms hyperactivity, helps one to be more fertile.

CINNABAR — "Dragon's Blood" stone, protection from radiation.

CITRINE — Helps one define what they want from life. Good for the circulation, and alleviates depression.

COPPER — Gives strength to the body; some say copper bracelets alleviate arthritis pains. Draws moisture to the body; good for self-esteem and luck; helps energy flow.

CORAL — Enhances fertility. Protection from evil. A good stone for children (protects them); also signifies creative forces. Endows wisdom. **BROWN CORAL:** attracts evil spirits; **RED CORAL:** deep devotion.

CRYSTAL — Clarity of thought; wisdom; healing; communicating. Reveals secrets of the future and power; gives one power over one's own life.

DIAMOND — If a diamond is clear, love is true; if cloudy, tainted. Makes one immune from poisons, Save one from bad dreams. Good to wear during confrontations: gives superior strength. Regarded by some to be the most powerful stone, it symbolizes the sun and invisible fire. Helps to cure eye diseases.

EMERALD — Said to make the owner a cleaner and more organized person; eases childbirth pain and epileptic seizures. Used to divine future (staring into stone enhances clairvoyance); also helpful for dream divination; enhances intelligence and memory. If an emerald is near, no evil eye will work. Brings strength to the aged. Never should be given as a gift on Monday, when it's unlucky; best if given on a Wednesday. If love is true, this stone is bright. As love fades, so does the emerald.

FLUORITE — Negates the effects of crystals. On its own: enhances "third eye" powers.

THE BEST LITTLE BEADING BOOK

GARNET — Very powerful; bestows friendship, generosity, and long life. Clears skin disorders (acne), aleviates swelling, promotes creativity. Protection from bad wishes, talisman and protection from wounds and evil. When worn, gives true love, faithfulness.

GLASS — Blue glass beads ward off the evil eye.

GOLD — Virtue, generosity, energy, and luck; new opportunities. Golden circles are the most powerful; gold signifies the sun. Gold strengthens due to its ability to conduct electricity, it has a high energy value. It's believed that one can rub an eye with a gold ring to cure a sty. Gold jewelry prolongs labor (doctors used to tell women to remove their gold jewelry before labor).

HEMATITE — "Hema" means blood: improves quality of blood; enhances memory; heightens vitality. The high iron content can help decrease anemia and menstrual cramping.

HORN — Protects from evil eye.

IRON — Worn around the neck, it wards off the evil eye. In some places, people knock iron the way some knock wood for good luck. A cross made of iron protects from evil and the supernatural. Wearing iron keeps one healthy and attracts positive forces. Iron gives balance, endurance, longevity, and efficiency.

IVORY — Keeps away evil spirits.

JADE — (Jadeite and Nephrite) Eases thirst; aids kidney and spleen function, good for the eyes. Sometimes called "The Kidney Stone". Can bring on rain; protection from lightning. Eases pain in childbirth, repells wild animals, improves dreams, and gives feeling of calmness. Makes pregnancy easier, and makes a home peaceful. A very positive stone, it regenerates the life force and promotes attunement with nature. Brings one closer to perfection.

JASPER — **GREEN JASPER** brings on rain, helps restore sense of smell; **RED JASPER** stops bleeding; helps one breathe easier; helps in childbirth.

JET — Renders spells and curses useless. Drives away snakes, heals headaches and toothaches. Worn by women in mourning (sometimes called "The Mourning Bead"). A cross made of jet is especially powerful for warding off the evil eye.

LAPIS LAZULI — If you wear lapis, you'll always be loved. Brings one closer to God. Relieves anxiety, good for the eyes; attracts good luck. Lapis mixed with crystal gives great power. Believed to be the 11th stone of the Breastplate. Sometimes called "The Stone of Heaven", it's believed that the 10 Commandments were carved on lapis.

MALACHITE — Eases childbirth pains; protects young children and eases their pain in cutting new teeth. Protection from the evil eye; heart-shaped malachite will bring healing to a broken heart.

MAGNETITE (LODESTONE) — Very magnetic and very powerful. Improves memory; helps hand and foot ailments; improves one's love life.

MOONSTONE — A very feminine stone; enhances E.S.P.; helps divine the future; lucky for lovers; promotes true love. Aids in childbirth [!]; eases nosebleeds and headaches; relieves swelling from fluids and helps fight cancer. Sometimes called "The Ceylon Opal", when mixed with pearls, it's extremely powerful. Can bring you to new experiences in life; helps those seeking spiritual guidance. Moonstone ranges from an orange-ish hue to milky white; as white is the most powerful of all colors, white Moonstone is considered the most powerful

OBSIDIAN — Purification, transformation, great inner strength in the face of adversity. Good for the eyes; gives insight. Being volcanic in origin, signifies fire, the life force, and creation. Representative of souls, both before and after life.

ONYX — Brings family discord, nightmares, sadness. Unlucky for lovers.

OPAL — Keeps blondes blonde longer (they don't get gray or white hair); Improves eyesight; sometimes makes the wearer go unnoticed. Some say it's unlucky, unless it's your birthstone (October); others say anyone can wear it if it's given as a gift in October. **BLACK OPAL:** brings good luck; **FIRE OPAL** brings hope and achievement (because of its colors, said to be the stone of children, the theatre, and all else light-hearted). Enhances clairvoyance when held on the forehead. Draws its owner into new situations.

PEARL — Innocence and fertility; thought to sometimes bring grief (called "The Tear Stone" and "Tears of the Sea"); mixing it with diamonds neutralizes this negative effect. Thought also to be an aphrodesiac, cure depression and insanity; brings long life; eases chest and heart pains; signifies truth and spiritual knowledge; preserves chastity; cools hot tempers; brings understanding; an introspective stone.

PERIDOT — Cures liver and intestinal ailments; Most powerful when set in gold; has a calming influence. When pierced with a hole, protects against evil.

PETRIFIED WOOD — Strength and wisdom, protection in later years.

PLATINUM — Conducts electricity; good for the heart; enhances clairvoyance.

PYRITE — Makes one more cheerful; helps speech; alleviates stuttering.

RHODOCHROSITE — Brings compassion and tenderness to one's life; also called "Inca Rosestone".

RHODONITE — Enhances language proficiency and gives calmness; protects the lungs.

ROCK CRYSTAL — Relieves thirst. Very powerful; used for crystal balls (very strong spiritually); brings rain; enhances communication and pureness of heart. Signifies infinity of space and time.

ROSE QUARTZ — A positive stone of an extremely gentle nature. Helps general well-being, and heart-related illnesses. Brings beauty to one's life.

RUBY — Extremely powerful; linked to the life force, fire, and blood. Good for the heart; keeps thoughts pure; creates positive forces and higher concentration. More powerful when worn on left side of body. It's said to be able to boil water.

SILVER — A feminine metal; enhances the power of one who wears it. It can never be touched by magic (that's why they use silver bullets and spikes in monster movies). Associated with the moon; cleanses the body of contamination and strengthens psychic abilities.

SAPPHIRE — Protection from evil and black magic. Brings truth, goodness, and purity. Heals eye ailments and other facial problems.

SARDONYX — Protects against bad thoughts and snake bites. Makes unlucky onyx less powerful; increases intelligence; and helps one make good choices.

SERPENTINE — Protection from snakes and their bites.

SMOKY QUARTZ — Gives power to one over their life; makes life's transitions easier.

SODALITE — Imparts calmness and strength. Lowers fevers and high blood pressure. Helps headaches and sinus problems.

SPINEL — Brings serenity and prosperity.

TIGER'S EYE — Promotes clear thinking, peace, courage,and self-confidence in one's physical being. Clarifies one's life by staring into it and reflecting on one's past deeds and future plans.

TOPAZ — Very sensitive to heat (changes color); said to deepen in color as the moon waxes. Protection from nightmares, epidemics, fear of death. Helps souls pass from this world to the next. Protection from attacks or injury.**BLUE TOPAZ** brings good thoughts and serenity. Helps one sleep peacefully; said to cool boiling water. **YELLOW TOPAZ** is most harmonious; can cure hemorrages.

TOURMALINE — Good luck; brings motivation and purpose; useful for meditation. **GREEN TOURMALINE:** is good for heart ailments; **WATERMELON TOURMALINE** brings insight and selfless love and compassion.

TURQUOISE — A stone very close to the basics of the earth; helpful to hunters; protection from injury; imparts wisdom, serenity, honesty, and friendship; brings happiness and good health; protection from evil eye. Aids meditation (a stone of growth). Protection from spiders and snake bites; improves health of eyes; best if turquoise is given as a gift.

ZIRCON — A good stone. Brings good dreams and peace; makes one happy, and is good for health. Alleviates childbirth pains. **HYACINTH ZIRCON:** provides safe travel, and helps chest pains; **YELLOW ZIRCON:** brings new love.

Gemstones and the Zodiac

The practice of matching birthstones to Zodiac signs dates back thousands of years. It's long been believed that, depending on your time of birth, certain stones were luckier for you than others.

January	Capricorn	Garnet
February	Aquarius	Amethyst
March	Pisces	Bloodstone or Aquamarine
April	Aries	Diamond
May	Taurus	Emerald
June	Gemini	Pearl or Moonstone
July	Cancer	Ruby
August	Leo	Peridot
September	Virgo	Sapphire
October	Libra	Opal or Tourmaline
November	Scorpio	Topaz or Citrine
December	Sagittarius	Turquoise

The Zodiac signs are divided into four groups: Fire, Earth, Water, and Air.

Fire Sign — Embodies power, energy, passion (Feeling). This includes Aries, Leo, and Sagittarius. Stones for this group include Carnelian, Obsidian, Ruby.

Earth Sign — Symbolizes adaptability, temperament, stubbornness (Sensation). This includes Capricorn, Taurus, and Virgo. Stones for this group include Agate, Jasper, Lapis, Malachite, and Turquoise.

Water Sign — Easy-going, emotional, caring (Intuition). This includes Pisces, Cancer, Scorpio. Stones for this group include Coral, Opal, and Pearl.

Air Sign — Intellectual, capable, progressive (Thinking). This includes Aquarius, Gemini, and Libra. Stones for this group include Aquamarine, Amethyst, and Crystal.

When creating jewelry, it's best to keep these environments in mind: Stones of the same sign work well together; mixing is a little trickier. Air complements Earth; Water complements Fire. Earth and Fire work well together; as does Air and Water.

There are also stones for each day of the week:

Sunday	Diamond
Monday	Pearl
Tuesday	Ruby
Wednesday	Amethyst
Thursday	Carnelian
Friday	Emerald
Saturday	Turquoise

In addition to the widely-known Zodiac, there is also the Chinese Zodiac. Rather than months, these symbols correlate to the birth year. It is said that Buddha promised rewards to all of the animals who would make the pilgrimage to see him. Of the entire animal kingdom, only twelve came: the dragon, the snake, the horse, the ram, the monkey, the rooster, the dog, the boar, the rat, the ox, the tiger, and the hare.

If you like to incorporate symbolic charms in your jewelry, these can give extra meaning to the shapes you choose to include in your pieces.

Year of the Dragon (1952, 1964, 1976, 1988)
People born under this sign are courageous, healthy, and gentle. They're sensitive, and great leaders.

Year of the Snake (1953, 1965, 1977, 1989)
People born this year have great wisdom. They have good luck with money, and are very attractive.

Year of the Horse (1954, 1966, 1978, 1990)
People in this sign are popular, cheerful, and talented.

Year of the Ram (1955, 1967, 1979, 1991)
People born under the sign of the Ram are very artistic, and appreciate beauty.

Year of the Monkey (1956, 1968, 1980, 1992)
People born under this sign are sensible, well-informed, and have great common sense. They are good decision makers.

Year of the Rooster (1957, 1969, 1981, 1993)
People born this year are deep thinkers, hard workers, and are very outspoken. They have many loyal friends and admirers.

Year of the Dog (1958, 1970, 1982, 1994)
Dog people are honest, loving, and very loyal. They are good at keeping secrets, and very fair.

Year of the Boar (1959, 1971, 1983, 1995)
People born under this sign are brave, polite, and shy. They make good friends, and have great inner strength.

Year of the Rat (1960, 1972, 1984, 1996)
People born this year are very charming. They have integrity and ambition.

Year of the Ox (1961, 1973, 1985, 1997)
Ox people are good friends. They listen well, and inspire others with their patience and calmness.

Year of the Tiger (1962, 1974, 1986, 1998)
People born under this sign plan well. They are respected by all who know them, and sought after as friends.

Year of the Hare (1963, 1975, 1987, 1999)
People born this year rarely get angry. They keep their promises, and are very lucky to be around.

Symbolism in Shapes

The practice of using shapes from nature in jewelry started in ancient times. Each has symbolic meaning. This is not just for metal trinkets that you may incorporate in your jewelry, but also the shapes of your beads. Here are some of the most common:

ACORNS — Abundance, fertility. A woman who wears beads of or in the shape of acorns will never grow old. Also, lightening can't strike you if you wear something of this shape.

ALMOND — Virginity.

AMULET — derives from the Arab word "hamala", which means "to carry". An amulet can be anything that is carried on the body at any time.

ANCHOR — Hope, stability, tenacity, tranquility.

ANKH — Eqyptian symbol of life and afterlife; immortality; all things in Creation.

ANT — Hard work.

ANTELOPE — Considered by many to be a holy animal, it symbolizes the Divinity and strength.

APE — To some, the ape symbolizes fun and levity; to others, it symbolizes sin and everything opposite God; to others, it represents gentleness and goodness; and lastly, to still others, the Monkey-God.

APPLE — Knowledge, self-awareness, fertility, temptation.

ARM — Sometimes used as a "milagro" (for purposes of healing); also means prayer, truth, and ability.

ARROW — A very masculine symbol, it means virility, strength, and war; linked in symbolism as a ray from the sun; vengence; light rays.

BALL — The sun and the moon; the power of the Gods; protection (round, like a Mandala). [Most beads used are round].

BAMBOO — Longevity, old friendship, strength in old age, happiness.

BAT — Darkness, wealth, sad restlessness.

BEADS — The continuous circle of beads symbolizes the cycle of life, prayer, and protection.

BEAR — New life, resurrection, strength, wisdom.

BEAR CLAW — Strength and ability..

BEE — Hard work, careful planning, immortality, purity, sweetness, wisdom, unselfishness.

BELL — Good vs. evil; protection from the evil eye.

BEETLE — Scarab; symbolizes eternal life. Literally, it represents male regeneration and fatherhood; stages of life and afterlife. Sometimes carved with "anch" (life), "ha" (increase of power), "tet" (stability), and "ur" (the afterlife).

BIRD — Gaiety, happiness, new beginnings, the soul.

BONE — Mortality and resurrection.

BOOK — Wisdom, Life's secrets.

BOTTLE — The womb.

BOX — The womb.

BROOM — Resilience and wisdom.

BULL — Masculine strength, the sun, royalty.

BUTTERFLY — Weathering life's changes; immortality; the soul. White butterflies bring happiness and good health; three butterflies together attract wealth.

CAMEL — Strength and endurance.

CAT — Freedom, strength, independence, good luck, and many friends.

CHAMELEON — Worn as a charm on a necklace, this brings protection from disease.

CHERRY — Fertility and sweetness.

CHILDREN — Hope for the future, new endeavors.

CIRCLE —Eternity; everything and one thing: wholeness. Karl Jung, the psychologist, wrote of the universal symbolism of the "Mandala" (circle), and how the concept of wholeness linked to the circle transcends culture and continent. A circle with a dot in the center represents the sun, and is linked with the number 10 (9 planets + 1 sun). Beads with this marking are called "Evil Eye" beads, because the evil eye can't penetrate their protection.

CLOUDS — Supernatural protection, a link with the life force.

COINS — (Money) with holes - very lucky, they keep away bad luck (i.e., Chinese coins). Coins made in the year of your birth are particularly lucky.

CORN — Fertility, gifts of the earth.

COW — Feminine nourishment.

COYOTE — The transformations of life; one who is strong and heroic, playfulness.

CRESCENT — Immortality.

CROSS — Besides Christian beliefs (the cross in reference to Jesus Christ), the cross is seen as the perfect symbol, with its 4 points (see the section on the number 4). A cross in a circle symbolizes the seasons, the "wheel of life" turning. Other interpretations of the cross include wisdom, great power, protection in childbirth, and a strong link with nature.

CUBE — Perfection.

DOG — Good friends, alertness, nobility.

DOLPHIN — Goodness, helpfulness, speed.

DOVE — Rebirth, peace, new beginnings, a messinger.

DRAGON — wildness, unfocused strength.

DUCK — Immortality.

EAGLE — The sun, masculine strength, the earth, a link with God.

EARTH — Motherhood (the Earthmother), nourishment, the body.

EGG — Fertility, the beginning of life, hope, afterlife.

ELEPHANT — Strength, remembrance, the sun.

EYE — Intuition, the sun and the moon, circles, vision, wisdom.

FAN — Life, nobility, air.

FEATHER — Universal truth, heaven, light and air.

FEET — Journey, humbleness..

FISH — Happiness, prosperity, fertility, Christianity.

FLOWER — Femininity, passiveness, receptiveness, beauty, love.

FROG — Fertility and bringing on rain.

GOAT — Masculinity, energy.

GOOSE — Happiness for family and home, love, air.

HAND — Hand of Fatima ("Hamsa"); signifies deeds; protection from evil eye; communication; an open hand means trust.

HARE (RABBIT) — Fertility; prosperity, regeneration and multiplying of one's resources.

HEAD — Life, wisdom, control.

HEART — Compassion, love, life, generosity.

HEN — Motherhood.

HORN — Protection from evil eye, supernatural powers, protection, royalty.

HORSE — Earthly power, fertility. White horses are particularly lucky, and signify strength.

HORSESHOE — Good luck, protection from evil spirits. Rubbing two horseshoes together brings luck.

KEY — A masculine form; symbolic of home, power, riches, unlocking of truth and mysteries.

KNIFE — Masculinity, strength, keeps away Satan.

KNOT — Eternal life, wisdom, linked with Buddha as a symbol of goodness and power.

LADYBUG — Femininity, home, good luck.

LEAF — New opportunities; happy days, growth.

LIGHTNING — Enlighenment, heavenly revelations, destruction, masculinity, great changes.

LION — Linked to the power of the sun, it symbolizes masculinity, animal desires, strength, lack of compassion.

MANDALA — Circle (within a circle), wholeness, the world, the universe, all Creation, the door to heaven, inner strength, and sacred places.

MONKEY — See ape.

MOON — Eternity, enlightenment, femininity, the soul, peace, phases of nature. Luckiest in crescent shape; very lucky when paired with star; particularly lucky for women.

MOUSE — Strength in the small, children.

MUSHROOM — Fertility; aphrodesiac.

NECKLACE — Dignity, continuity. When beads are strung in a necklace, they symbolize the subservient nature of man and all living things to God. The first necklaces represented the link of man to God. Man was represented by the beads, God as the thread that holds us together.

OCTAGON — Regeneration, the cycle of life.

OUROBOROS — A serpent that eats its own tail, it's a universal symbol for "in the end, there is the beginning". With the power of the circle, it embodies self-sufficiency, strength, nature, the universe, and one-ness.

OWL — In Native American legends, the owl is the one who brings the soul to heaven. Represents rebirth and wisdom.

PARROT — Gaiety, superficial and unoriginal thought.

PI — "Annular" shape, considered the door to heaven. It is believed that when prayers are whispered through the hole in the Pi, they are answered.

PLANTS — Growth, new opportunities, changes.

RAINBOW — Evidence of God's love, all things (as evidenced by all colors).

ROCK — (Nuggets/irregular shaped); permanence, strength.

ROSE — Eternity, fertility, secrets, attracts love.

SCARAB — Eternal life, the sun, male regeneration.

SNAKES — Regeneration, tenacity, the sun, strength. Rattles signify good luck.

STAR — The presence of a diety, eternal life, hope, a symbol of angels (God's messengers). Grants wishes, especially stars made of gold. Four stars in a row signify new love.

STONES — Symbolic of the soul, some people feel a natural connection with stones and collect them wherever they go. There is a beach in Hawaii where it is forbidden to take the stones, as they embody of the souls of the dead ancestors of the people who live near by. Some stones are considered sacred.

STRING / THREAD — Associated with life; knotted string signifies protection from death.

SUN — Birth and strength, masculine power, the number one.

TEETH — Good luck and courage, aggression.

TIGER — Same in symbolism as lion.

TREE — Life, growth, wisdom, the coming together of air, earth, and water.

TRIANGLE — Completion, the universe, the body, all the power of the number three. Two triangles together make the Star of David.

UNICORN — The moon, femininity, protection, gentleness, compassion, inner strength.

WALNUT — Fertility, strength.

WAVES / WATER — Change, the ebb and tide of life, the source of life, the essence of what is needed, all things.

WISHBONE — Luck and marriage.

WOLF — Fierceness, base desires, the earth, strength.

Color

There are three primary colors: red, yellow, and blue. Secondary colors (made from mixing the primaries) are purple, orange and green. On the color wheel, the colors directly opposite each other are called Complementary Colors. All colors come from the primaries (in varying ratios) and black and white. Black is the absence of color, and white is the presence of all colors (A prism separates out the spectrum from white light).

Behavioral scientists have long been aware of the effect color has on people. It's believed that the use of color can alter moods, alleviate tension, give protection, and heal, among other things. There are cultural connotations of color for holidays (red/green: Christmas; black/orange: Halloween, etc.). Studies have shown that color preferences can be gender-based (women like blue-based reds, while men prefer yellow-based reds). We equate color with cost (green is considered an "expensive" color, while orange is considered "cheap").

Color reflects where we live, and the seasons of the year. A friend of mine who is Native American told me that Native American bead artists in the north (where days are shorter) use darker colors in their beadwork, rather than the bright colors used in the "Sun Belt" of the Southwest, where days are longer and hotter.

Nearly everyone has had their "colors" done, and have their favorite tones to wear, based on the seasons of the year. Rust and earth tones for fall (warm colors); contrasty, cold colors for winter (black, white, silver); pastels and "sweet" colors for Spring (cool); and bright, hot colors for summer.

If you are aware of the power and meanings of colors, you can use that to your advantage when designing your jewelry.

PRIMARY COLORS are the most powerful, associated with strength (Superheroes' costumes are always primary colors).

MIXING COMPLEMENTARY COLORS creates excitement and energy.

YELLOWS AND ORANGES denote warmth and light.

BLUES AND GREENS denote soothing influences and coolness.

PURPLES mixed with blues give the illusion of mystery and the unknown.

Some common beliefs of the meanings of colors are:

BLACK - is a protective color. It absorbs negative influences and protects the wearer. It repels negativity.

WHITE - is strength. It derives its power from all colors, which it contains. Denotes strength of the spirit, also innocence and purity.

RED - is raw energy, fire, life. Red is protection from the evil eye, and lifts your spirits. It's love, magnetism, and good luck.

SCARLET RED - Emotion, anger.

DEEP CRIMSON - Animal-like passion.

BRIGHT RED - Courage, confidence.

ORANGE -Vitality, success, friendship, attraction, adaptability. The fire of red, tempered with the logic of yellow.

YELLOW - Self awareness and knowledge. Success, creativity, quick luck, activity, and intelligence. Considered unlucky for actors. Yellow is the color of feminine strength.

LIGHT YELLOW - Common sense.

GREEN - Growth, the earth. Love and hope, and generosity. Green is compassion, healing and growth, good health. Green is also considered lucky to attract money, and is unlucky on Thursday.

BLUE - Serenity, calmness, good health, truth, harmony at home. Blue is considered "Heaven's Color".

INDIGO -Wisdom, to know all; to gain insight.

VIOLET - Leadership, enlightenment, understanding. The spirit at its best, overcoming bad habits. Power, high energy, high honors, progress, motivation, self control.

BROWN - Worldly wisdom.

PINK - Femininity, sweetness, youth, love, affection, unselfishness.

•••••

Lucky colors have been associated with different days of the week.

MONDAY	Blue	Hopeful Day
TUESDAY	Pink	True Love Day
WEDNESDAY	Yellow	Wisdom Day
THURSDAY	Orange	Intuition Day
FRIDAY	Green	Lucky Day
SATURDAY	Black & White	Organization Day
SUNDAY	Orchid (Lavender)	Spirituality Day

●●●●●

Color combinations come in and out of vogue. There are many designer guide books available to help you put colors together in new and exciting ways. Here are some combinations from the past:

Platinum/Pearl Tones - The thirties.
Bold Polka Dots/Geometric Shapes in Red - The forties.
Yellow / Navy Blue - The late-forties to early fifties.
Black / Red - The fifties.
Pink / Gray - The fifties.
Avocado Green / Gold - The sixties.
Shocking Pink / Orange - The sixties.
Black / White - The sixties.
Red / White / Blue - The early seventies.
Chocolate Brown / Camel - The seventies.
Denim Blue / Dusty Rose - The seventies.
Hunter Green / Camel - The eighties.
"Jewel Tones" Mixed - The eighties.
Burgundy / Gray - The eighties.
New Wave Hot Pink / Black - The eighties.
Black / Purple / Green - The late eighties.
Pink / Green - The nineties.
Terracotta / Pale Green - The nineties.
Purples / Greens / Blues - The nineties.
Hot Pink / Bright Orange / Chartreuse (Day-Glo) - The nineties.
Turquoise / Rust - The nineties.

Keep in mind, also . . . color is a very subjective thing. What is "sky-blue" to one person is "sea-blue" to another. Everyone reads color differently. If you are designing a piece of jewelry to match an item of clothing or another piece of jewelry, it is best to have some kind of swatch of color. My favorite swatch system costs nothing, yet is very effective. Hardware stores have paint swatch cards that are free. It is very easy to find them in the colors that match your beads. Cut them out into little rectangles of color. When designing a piece, you can play with the little swatches until you find a combination that is pleasing. If you number them on the back (i.e., RQ1 could be Rose Quartz 1, etc.) you have a reference that you can record as to what colors were used in a particular piece of jewelry.

THE BEST LITTLE BEADING BOOK

Lucky Numbers

When designing a piece, I take every aspect into consideration: the colors, the intended wearer's birthsign, the shapes and meanings of the beads, even the number of strands or other key numbers of elements in the piece. Here are some general ideas about numbers.

ONE — One is lucky; the supreme, dominant number that represents the sun, God, and life. When designing a necklace, one large focal point will make a more dramatic, powerful necklace then several smaller.

TWO — Two is a feminine number; a very democratic number. It represents balance, cooperation, and couples. If you have two of something, they are usual equal in importance (i.e., twins).

THREE — Three is mystic and an extremely lucky number. It signifies perfection, triangles (i.e., the Divine Trinity), and protection from evil. Occurrences happen (usually) in threes.

FOUR — The number of nature: 4 seasons; 4 elements (earth, fire, water, and air); 4 corners of the earth.

FIVE — An inconsistent number: it's associated with boldness and daring; but also erratic-ness. Five is very sensual (i.e., the five senses), and signifies love, marriage, and passion. Five is said to ward off evil, and give protection from bad luck.

SIX — Signifies Creation (it's the sum total of 1 + 2 + 3), it equals all that precedes it. Some consider it to be the most perfect and stable number. It brings beauty, harmony, and balance. There are six points on the Star of David.

SEVEN — A mystic, very powerful number. Regarded by some to the the perfect spiritual number, most find it lucky. God created the earth in 7 days; there are 7 deadly sins. It is the number of intellectual strength.

EIGHT — Not an artistic number, it signifies success in business, and great strength. It is a very materialistic number.

NINE — Some consider it sacred, as it is three times three (symbolizing the Trinity at its most powerful). Nine symbolizes love, permanance, and fertility (human pregnancies last 9 months).

TEN — A combination of one (the supreme) and zero (nothing), it symbolizes harmony and balance.

ELEVEN — Considered to be lucky, it symbolizes fairness and equality.

TWELVE — Considered to be a very "mortal" number, it is preoccupied with time: 12 months, 12 hours.

THIRTEEN — Considered very unlucky almost everywhere, in certain places (i.e., Italy), it is considered the luckiest of all numbers.

TWENTY-ONE — A lucky number, and very powerful (comprised of three times seven).

TWENTY-THREE — Some regard this as unlucky, leading to overindulgences.

• • • • • • •

If you wish to find your own personal lucky number, you take the letters of your name, and, using the table below, add them up. Keep adding them until they are a one-digit number (see example). This is your lucky number.

1	2	3	4	5	6	7	8	9
A	B	C	D	E	F	G	H	I
J	K	L	M	N	O	P	Q	R
S	T	U	V	W	X	Y	Z	

J	A	N	E		D	O	E
1	1	5	5		4	6	5

$$1 + 1 + 5 + 5 + 4 + 6 + 5 = 27$$

$$2 + 7 = 9.$$

Jane Doe's lucky number would be 9.

Some General Superstitions About Jewelry

Everyone has heard them: those "Old Wives' Tales". Sometimes they're silly, sometimes obscure, but always fun. Here are a few popular ones.

- If you wear jade, it becomes part of you.
- If you break a strand of beads and don't collect them all, you'll have bad luck.
- Buttons are lucky to give as gifts.
- If the clasp of a necklace comes around the front, (a) someone is thinking of you, or (b) you get your wish.
- If you want true friends, wear a topaz.
- If you find spiders, gold is nearby.
- Never BUY good luck charms — they lose their power when money changes hands.
- Turquoise charm stones, when worn around the neck, are good luck.
- If you break a strand of pearls and don't collect all of them, your family will scatter.
- Wearing black beads enhances your love life.
- Amber beads kill sexual desire.
- If you rub black onyx on a wart, throw the stone over your left shoulder, and don't look back, the wart will go away.
- Uranium under the bed cures rheumatism.
- Rubies cure rheumatism.
- A string of beads with a tassel at the end are good luck.
- If you bring onyx into the house, they'll be a quarrel.
- Circles enclose good luck.
- A gold ring on your left hand guards against leprosy.
- Copper draws fluid from the body.
- Lead worn around the neck on a silver chain prevents nosebleeds.
- Magnets draw rheumatism from the joints.
- A brass ring gets rid of rheumatism.
- If you wear lapiz, you'll always be loved.

Bead Tales

This section is a mixture of anecdotes, true stories, and just plain silliness that pertains to beads. As you know, when you love beads, there's more to them than just stringing them. There's looking at them, hearing about them, hunting for them, and much, much more.

The Entrepreneur

This is a true story about the resourcefulness of one of my students.

Andrea* went through a very difficult divorce. Her ex-husband paid no child support for their two young children. Finding it hard to get a decent job, she was forced to go on welfare.

Andrea joined one of my vocational jewelry making classes. She took to making peyote and comanche stitch earrings immediately. She could whip out 20-30 pairs a day, with no problems whatsoever.

Economics in the area were difficult, and she realized she had to come up with a market where she could sell her jewelry with little or no competition.

Andrea found the perfect place to sell her exotic and beautiful earrings: Topless bars.

She would bring several cases of earrings to each bar. The dancers loved them (as Andrea said, "They didn't clash with anything"). The spectators would buy them to take home to their wives. Everyone was happy — especially Andrea, who was making money hand-over-fist!

Andrea is no longer on welfare. She's doing very well with her earrings, and her very unique market!

She asked me not to use her real name.

A Trip to the Bead Store

(With Apologies to Dr. Seuss)

When coming from work one day,
Betsy O'Dimm
Spotted a bead store
And went in on a whim

"I'd love a new necklace,"
She thought with a gloat.
"Something to go with my
Pretty new coat."

When she stepped in the bead store,
Her eyes popped from her head . . .
There were beads that were purple,
There were beads that were red.

There were beads made of quartz,
There were beads made of stone,
There were beads made of glass,
And some out of bone.

"Let me help you, my dear,"
The saleslady said with a grin.
Ah, but that's when Betsy's head
Really started to spin!

"To make the right necklace,
You'll need lots of beads.
They should match your cottons,
They should match your tweeds.

"They should be bright colors,
They should be quite bold.
They should make you look pretty,
Not dreary and old.

"Now, you'll need thread,
I think silk will do.
Let me think . . . let me think . . .
Is this one strand or two?

"Now, you'll need knot covers,
Don't forget, you need glue,
And a nice fancy clasp,
Something glitzy and new.

"And, of course, you'll need earrings,"
The saleslady said,
As she tossed on the eyepins,
The earwires, more thread.

Betsy got so excited,
She thought she'd expire!
"Hand me the nymo!
Hand me a plier!

"Give me a tweezers,
A bead board and tape,
Some seedbeads, some bugles,
Ah, it's taking shape!"

Ms. O'Dimm's fingers flew
As she beaded like heck . . .
The mountains of beads
Encircled her neck.

The red beads, the blue ones,
They glimmered and shined,
The fetish, the clasp,
The strands intertwined.

With a skip in her step,
Betsy left the bead store,
But, I saw the glint in her eye . . .
She'll be back for more!

If you really loved your beads, you'd name your next child after them, right? (huh?!) This is a list of names (and meanings) that will remind you of your favorite beads (or children).

GIRLS' NAMES

Adamina — "red earth"
Amber — "jewel"
Amethyst — "a jewel"
Antonia — "a priceless jewel"
Aurelia — "golden"
Aurora — "glowing"
Beryl — "precious jewel of the sea"
Cameo — "a jewel that is sculpted"
Cara — "precious little jewel"
Chryseis — "daughter of gold"
Cobalta — "from a blue place"
Coral — "sea jewel"
Cordelia — "sea jewel"
Crystal — "clear visioned"
Diamanta — "diamond"
Dore — "of gold"
Dorene — "golden girl"
Eartha — "of the earth"
Ebony — "dark beautiful one"
Emeralda — "beautiful green jewel"
Esmeralda — "emerald"
Gemma — "precious gem"
Galatea — "milky, white jewel (ivory)"
Garnet — "gem"
Gilda — "gold-covered"
Gina — "silver girl"
Hermione — "of the earth"

Hertha — "earth mother"
Ijada — "jade"
Iona — "purple jewel"
Ivory — "pure"
Jade — "perfection"
Jewel — "precious one"
Margaret — "a pearl"
Marjorie — "a pearl"
Opal — "jewel"
Ora — "gold"
Oriana — "golden one"
Orlena — "the golden girl"
Parnella — "little rock"
Pearl — "precious gem"
Pegeen — "pearl"
Petra — "rock"
Rita — "a pearl"
Rochelle — "of the little rock"
Rohana — "sandlewood"
Roxanne — "brilliant gem"
Ruby — "precious red stone"
Sapphire — "beautiful one"
Sorcha — "bright stone"
Topaz — "gem"
Tourmaline — "pretty gem"
Ula — "red jewel"

THE BEST LITTLE BEADING BOOK

BOYS' NAMES

Adam — "red earth"
Arthur — "strong as a rock"
Carnelian — "horn"
Clay — "from the earth"
Clyde — "a rocky presence"
Collier — "one who mines"
Cornelius — "the color of horn"
Craig "of the stony hill"
Damek — "red earth"
Demetrius — "lover of stones"
Diamond — "strong one"
Doane — "one who lives in sand"
Eben — "stone"
Ebenezer — "stone of help"
Flint — "bright & strong"
Gaspar — "bringer of treasures
        (one of the Wisemen)"
Jasper — "treasure"
Kane — "radiant"
Kerwin — "jet / coal"
Macadam — "son of the red earth"
Mason — "one who works with stone"

Maynard — "strong as a rock"
Nuri — "stone made of fire"
Peter — "strong as a rock"
Phineas — "mouth of brass"
Pierce — "rock or stone"
Rochester — "rocky fortress"
Rock — "from a stone"
Rockley — "from a rocky meadow"
Rockwell — "from a stony well"
Skerry — "from the rocky isles"
Stamford — "of the rocky place"
Stanford — "from a stony crossing"
Stanton — "of a stony place"
Stancliff — "from a stony cliff"
Stein — "stone"
Sterling — "genuine"
Stinson — "son of stone"
Thurston — "Thor's stone (jewel)"
Tremaine — "one who lives in stone"
Tyler — "one who works with stone"
Telford — "one who makes jewelry"
Zuriel — "God is my rock"

Coral . . . A Surgeon's Best Friend

Recently, surgeons made a very surprising discovery. While searching for a material to help bones mend, they discovered that implanting coral is one of the best methods. Coral is very much like bone tissue, in that it has a high amount of calcium and many interconnecting tunnelways for nerves, vessels, etc.

They treat the coral to kill organisms, and the body accepts the coral just as it would bone (it's not rejected). After these grafts, healing takes place very rapidly.

THE BEST LITTLE BEADING BOOK

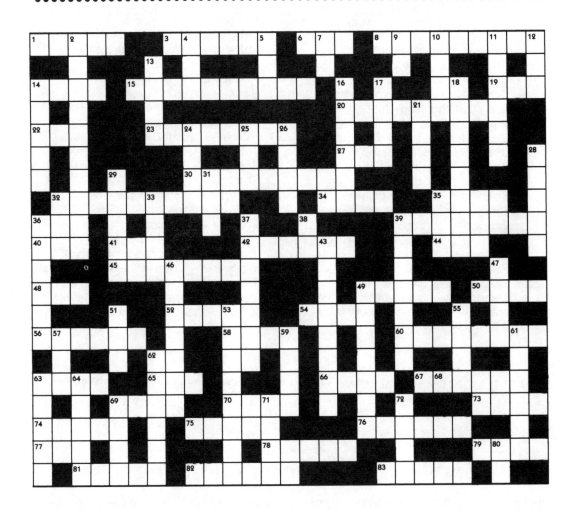

ACROSS

1. Small, drilled spheres
3. The shine on pearls; metallic or glossy finish on glass beads
6. Used for covering knots, either a knot cover or knot _____
8. Island purchased for $24 in beads

14. Very tiny beads measured in "aughts"
15. Pink member of quartz family
19. When doing beadwork, it's best not to stand, but to _____ (position)
20. Sometimes called "Indian Beads" or "Crow Beads"
22. Shiny, satiny ribbon sometimes used for stringing, _____ tail
23. Light bulbs that cause reddish coloration in finished photos
27. Animal that signifies freedom, strength, independence, and good luck
30. Type of bead that shortened the author's labor
32. Bead-making technique, literally means "a thousand flowers"
34. Sometimes called "Indian Beads", or "Pony Beads"
35. Long, thin strand of metal used for wrapping, making eyepins, etc.
36. This lady always carries a Rosary
39. Purple member of quartz family
40. There are two types of pins: head pins and _____ pins
41. The solar center of the universe
42. Small, disc shaped beads which come in brass or shell
44. The "mourning bead"
45. Blue stone sometimes mistaken for lapiz
48. Torpedo-shaped, inscribed bead originally from Tibet
49. What's on the ends of most necklaces
50. Very popular beads of the sixties, _____ beads
52. Very light bead, sometimes looks like plastic, a natural resin
54. Very elegant green semiprecious beads
56. Popular design in jewelry, imitates less-sophisicated styles
58. Used for weaving seedbeads
60. Extremely helpful for pearl knotting
62. Opposite of don't
63. Put this on the end of multiple strands to hide the knots
64. Number that signifies the sun, God, and life
66. Some projects take a lot of _____ to finish
67. Tool used for almost everything
69. Looks like ivory, but usually from camels
70. Beautiful brown when made into beads, usually derived from antelope
73. Varities of this stone include Blue and Fire _____
74. Looks like diamonds, but with painted backs, _____stones
75. _____ beads, used to barter in Africa
76. Small beads with "teeth" inside
77. We don't want just SOME beads, we want them _____
78. What's in an oyster
79. Very elegant, it's really chalcedony dyed black, but everyone calls it _____
81. Satiny finish on glass beads, sometimes called "chicklet" or "_____"
82. Small carved animal used with turquoise
83. When it's blue, it looks like aquamarine, it also comes in a smoky color

DOWN

2. Green member of quartz family
4. Never throw anything away . . . someday you'll _____ it
5. Where an earring goes
7. One inscription on scarab
9. Scientific abbreviation for gold
10. Opposite of love
11. Gathered strands of beads or threads, tied together at top, left free at bottom
12. Technique of weaving a necklace (interwoven)
13. Type of earring that goes through the ear and has a nut or clutch on the back
14. Unpierced type of earring with threaded post for adjusting pressure, _____ back
16. Used for spacing beads evenly apart
17. What goes in the knot cup
18. Plastic-like material that was very popular for jewelry in the 30's, 40's, and 50's
21. Used on a necklace for hanging pendants
24. Type of thread on small spool used for earrings
25. Another name for ecru (color)
26. Used like clutches on the back of a post earring
28. A form of chalcedony, it includes blue lace and botswana
29. _____ beads from the Czech Republic are the finest
31. Raw mineral or rock from which the good stuff is extracted
32. _____ bueno (very good)
33. When you lose a bead and cannot _____ it
36. Sometimes twisted wire, sometimes sized, "sharps" is one kind
37. Red, white and blue bead with zig-zag edging
38. This book _____ informative
39. Little bronze masks from Africa
43. Blood is in its name, and it scratches red
46. Type of shell that is used for jewelry, sometimes it's dyed
47. A cabochon is a flat-back, _____-front stone
49. Method of creating beads which involves firing in a kiln
51. Eye and head_____
53. One source of ivory
55. Not precious, but _____-precious
57. The twin number
59. Silver is symbolic of this heavenly body
61. Strand of beads used for prayer
62. Blue-green bead used on horse-carts
63. Skeletal remains of undersea creatures
64. Some manicurists imbed gems in these
69. Some end caps are shaped like the Liberty _____
71. Every artist wants them to sell their art (abbreviation)
72. Polymer made by Eberhart-Faber
80. Will we ever stop beading? The answer is _____!!!

ANSWERS TO CROSSWORD PUZZLE

ACROSS

1. Beads
3. Lustre
6. Cup
8. Manhattan
14. Seed
15. Rose Quartz
19. Sit
20. Ponybeads
22. Rat
23. Tungsten
27. Cat
30. Moonstone
32. Millifiore
34. Crow
35. Wire
36. Nun

39. Amethyst
40. eye
41. Sun
42. Heishe
44. Jet
45. Sodalite
48. Dzi
49. Clasp
50. Love
52. Amber
54. Jade
56. Ethnic
58. Loom
60. Tweezers
62. Do
63. Cone

64. One
66. Time
67. Pliers
69. Bone
70. Horn
73. Opal
74. Rhine
75. Trade
76. Crimps
77. All
78. Pearl
79. Onyx
81. Silky
82. Fetish
83. Topaz

DOWN

2. Aventurine
4. Use
5. Ear
7. Ur
9. Au
10. Hate
11. Tassel
12. Net
13. Post
14. Screw
16. Spacer
17. Knot
18. Bakelite
21. Bail
24. Nymo

25. Tan
26. Nuts
28. Agate
29. Glass
31. Ore
32. Muy
33. Find
36. Needle
37. Chevron
38. Is
39. Ashanti
43. Hematite
46. Abalone
47. Dome
49. Ceramic

51. Pin
53. Elephant
55. Semi
57. Two
59. Moon
61. Rosary
62. Donkey
63. Coral
64. Nails
69. Bell
71. Reps (abbrev. for Representatives)
72. Fimo®
80. No!!!!!

The Lady and the Snake

One of my students told me this story. I found it utterly delightful.

Living in a remote area was an 87-year-old, **extremely** self-sufficient woman. Being of Scottish decent, she was also very thrifty. She delighted in finding uses for everything.

Well, one summer she found herself being plagued by rattlesnakes. They were everywhere. So, she invested in a good hatchet. Midday, when the snakes were out sunning themselves, this energetic lady would sneak up on them and chop off their heads. She would then boil the body and eat the meat (she said it tasted like chicken).

Pretty soon, the rattlesnake bones started to pile up. So, being a clever and inventive person, she started stringing jewelry with them. It wasn't long before people started coming from miles around to buy these exotic necklaces — you see, she mixed the bones with fine crystal and antique beads. The combination was very beautiful, as well as startling.

Well, one day her older sister was coming for a visit. As she was nearing the house in her car, she spied a snake crossing the dirt road. She ran it over, but still it kept going. She backed the car over it, and still it continued on. Back and forth, back and forth, over the snake she went, but **still** it persisted. Finally, she parked the car on top of it, and ran up the road to get her sister. The two returned with the hatchet, and neatly chopped off the snake's head. While putting the parts in a grocery bag, the younger sister's hand brushed a fang of the snake. Well, even though the snake was dead, there was still venom in its fangs. Luckily, no real damage occurred. Her fingers turned blue for a day or so, then she was fine.

The two ladies are still alive, and our talented one is still killing, cooking, and creating with her snakes.

Does this sound unreal? Do you think it's fiction? Judge for yourself! Here's the proof: necklaces made from snake bones.

THE BEST LITTLE BEADING BOOK

A Confession

My name is Wendy, and, ah . . . I am a Beadaholic. Oh, it all started innocently enough. As a child, I was aware of the beads that the adults around me were addicted to. But it wasn't until a well-meaning relative decided to corrupt me with the family vice, that my own dependence took hold. I was given a present, and, being a child, I couldn't comprehend the danger of such an act. I eagerly unwrapped it. Inside was a kit to make your own Indian beaded rings on wire. When my fingers came into contact with the beads in the kit, I immediately felt a rush . . . my ears rang, I saw stars, the room reeled. With that one gift, my whole life changed. A lifelong addiction began.

I've heard it was the same for other Beadaholics . . . starting at very young ages. I knew I had a genetic pre-disposition (my grandmother was a Beadaholic), but my mother had her habit in control, and I hoped I had that strength.

Ah, but I've been weak. In my school years, I was caught several times illegally stringing love beads. Even though there were stiff consequences, my addiction could not, **would not** subside. As an adult, with a checkbook of my own, believe me, I've paid the price.

How many nights have I fed my family macaroni and cheese because I spent our food allowance on beads? How many bags of beads have I sneaked into the house, so no one knew? How many bags of beads have I hid in the car (under the seats, in the glove box)?

Oh, I have it bad. This is an obsession. I tried to rationalize it to myself and my husband . . . "Karl Jung said the circle is the symbol of wholeness. Most beads are round. I buy them because I'm searching for my whole self." or "The stones have healing power. By collecting them, it contributes to my psychic wellness." I tell him "Be happy I like to make my own jewelry. If I were the kind of woman who desired beautiful things and you had to buy them for me, we'd **really** be poor." Yes, you can imagine his responses.

Being a genetic disease, I have passed this on to my children. In the gem shows, you can hear their pitiful cries of "Buy me that" and "I would like one of those." Together, the three of us make a pitiful sight.

Ah, those gem shows. How many times have I run out of gas in my car because I spent my last nickel at the gem shows? As I enter one, I break into a cold sweat. Everything is irresistible. Everything is wonderful. I want it all. I **must have** it all. So, I buy a shopping bag full of beads, go home, and set it down next to the other full shopping bags I haven't yet had a chance to sort. I have a house full of beads. No matter how much I have, it's never enough. It's like the movie, "The Red Shoes", except it's beads, not dancing.

Do I have a fetish? Actually, I have several. Most of them are made out of turquoise.

I'm hooked. I've even been driven to experimenting with stronger things . . . yes, those rumors are true. Try Fimo once and you are addicted for life.

I'm in a support group with other Beadaholics, but sometimes we get sidetracked. We thrill in each other's stories of bead bargains and great finds. Sometimes we leave there longing for beads more than when we arrived.

I've tried to go cold turkey, but found myself making analogies between beads and food. Have you ever noticed how cherry cough drops look like garnets? And how many foods are round? I had to eliminate olives, cherries, and grapes from my diet for obvious reasons.

So, now I realize there is no peace. I accept my addiction, and try very hard to keep it under control. I feel . . . ah, . . . excuse me, ma'am, may I see your necklace? Where **did** you get those beads? A new bead store? Where? Ah, I've got to go now . . . something urgent just came up.

Index

Introduction 3
Jennie's Beadwork 5

BASIC INFORMATION
Measurements 10
Bead and Cabochon Sizes 11
Seed & Bugle Bead Sizes 12
Bead Shapes / Cuts / Surfaces 15
Types of Beads 23
How to Know What You're Buying 27
Findings 29
Chain Shapes 31
Stringing Media 32
Needles 35
Pliers 36
Anatomy of a Bead Box 37
Glues & Cements 38
Paints & Dyes 40
Design Fundamentals 42
Idea Sources 48
Full Color Photos 49-72
Color Photo Index 73

STEP BY STEP INSTRUCTIONS

WORKING WITH WIRE
Simple Earrings 74
Variations of Simple Earrings 76
Looped Wire Earrings 77
Wire Chain Necklaces 79
Rosaries 81
Charm Necklaces 83
Using Jump Rings 84
Wire Rings 85
Memory Wire 88
Wire Bending 90

STRINGING PROJECTS
Basic Stringing — Single Strand 93
Daisy Necklace 98
Leaf Necklace 100
Variations 101
Adjustable Length Necklace 103
Eyeglass Holders 105
Bead Knotting 106
Working With Bullion 113
The Magic Clasp 114
Combining Tiger Tail with Thread 116
Continuous Necklaces 118

MULTISTRAND NECKLACES
Multistrand Necklaces 121
Multistrand Seedbead Necklace 129
Southwestern Seedbead Necklace 130
Faux Zuni Necklace 131
Turquoise Necklace 132
Southwestern Charm Necklaces 133
Native American Collar 135
African Ashanti Necklace 137
Garnet & Citrine Necklace 139
Amethyst & Pearl Collar 140
BEADWEAVING
Needlewoven Charm Bracelet 143
Needlewoven Charm Necklace 147
Woven Crystal Necklace 148
Double Strand Bracelet 150
Pink Crystal Necklace 151
Red Crystal Collar 153
Woven Crystal Collar 155
Woven Semiprecious Necklace 158
WATCHBANDS
Watchbands 160
The Southwest Watchband 161
The Woven Watchband 164
The Twenty-Minute Watchband 165
The Bent Wire Watchband 166
The "Bubbly" Watchband 167
The Peyote Stitch Watchband 168
BEADING ON FABRIC
Beading on Fabric 169
Machine Beading 172
Beaded Brooch 173
COMBINATION NECKLACES
Medallion Necklace 174
Fantasy Necklace 175
Zucchini Necklace 176
WORKING WITH LEATHER
Working With Leather 178
Pi/Leather Necklace 180
Leather Stamping 181
Beaded Moccasins 182
KNOTWORK
Knotted Cord Necklace 186
Trinket Tassel with Chinese Knotting 187
Knotwork Variations 190
SEEDBEADS
Working with Seedbeads 192
Fringing Techniques 194
Comanche Stitch Earrings 195
Comanche Stitch Variations 199
Huichol Earrings 200
Peyote Stitches 203
Peyote Stitch Vegetables 204
Medicine Pouch 205
Pi Woven Necklace 207
Beading a Bead 208

Netted Lace Stitch 209
Circular Ring Earrings 210
Rainbow Earring 211
On-Loom Weaving 212
Loomed Necklace (on Cover) 213
Basic Cabochon Earrings 214
Fringed Seedbead Necklace 218
Peyote Stitching Around a Cabochon 221
Peyote Stitch Spoon 222
Fringed Earrings 223
Dream Catcher Earrings 224
God's Eye Earrings 225
Earring Experiments 226
BEADMAKING
Working with Polymer Clay 227
Enhancing Wooden Beads 231
Other Handmade Beads 233
OTHER PROJECTS
Hat Pins 234
Alternative Assembling Techniques 236
Origami Earrings 237
PRACTICAL INFORMATION
Jewelry Styles 238
Creating a Portfolio 239
Starting a Business 241
THE ESOTERIC
Chakras 243
Meanings of Stones 245
Gemstones & the Zodiac 250
Symbolism in Shapes 252
Color 256
Lucky Numbers 259
General Superstitions 261
BEAD TALES
Bead Tales 263
Crossword Puzzle 266
Crossword Answers 269
INDEX 272